GLOVES OFF

MOSTLY TRUE STORIES FROM MY LIFE IN HOCKEY

BEHN WILSON

COPYRIGHT © 2026 BEHN WILSON

GLOVES OFF

Mostly True Stories from My Life in Hockey

FIRST EDITION

ISBN   978-1-5445-5126-5   *Hardcover*
       978-1-5445-5125-8   *Paperback*
       978-1-5445-5127-2   *Ebook*

GLOVES OFF

To Rita. Thanks for enduring me!

*To my parents, John and Jean. You were always my yardstick
of who I would like to be, and I miss you every day.*

To Ellie, Kristie, and VJ. I love you.

To Christian and Austin. You light up my life.

To my hockey friends and teammates. Thanks for the great memories.

*To all those who tried to punch me in the face. I have gratitude
for all the life experiences that have shaped me and hold
no grudges. Just kidding. You can go fuck yourselves.*

CONTENTS

OPENING PUNCHES 11

PART 1: I STARTED OFF AS A YOUNG CHILD

MY HOCKEY HEROES 19

MY OWN PERSONAL ICE RINK 25

DEFENDING AGAINST BULLIES 27

PART 2: JUNIOR HOCKEY: SHIT JUST GOT REAL

AT FIFTEEN YEARS OLD, SHIT *REALLY* GOT REAL.............................33

MOVING UP THE RANKS 37

HAZING IN KALAMAZOO 41

IS JUNIOR HOCKEY A REAL CAREER? 43

ROOM AND BOARD AND OLD CARS 45

DOUG WILSON ALMOST ENDED MY CAREER 47

DEEP THOUGHTS 1 51

WHO HAS TIME FOR SCHOOL?...55

PUCKS HURT 59

ALLERGIES SUCK..65

LEARNING TO FIGHT WAS MY SUPERPOWER 67

EMPLOYED AS AN ASSASSIN 71

THE NHL DRAFT: ALL THE MARBLES IN ONE DAY..........................75

PART 3: TURNING PRO IN PHILADELPHIA

I'M A FLYER—ALMOST 79

DEEP THOUGHTS 2 83

A FLY ON THE WALL 87

MY POWER PLAYS WITH CLARKE, BARBER, AND LEACH: A CAREER HIGHLIGHT 89

DEEP THOUGHTS 3 91

A MILESTONE I DIDN'T WANT TO ACHIEVE 93

DEEP THOUGHTS 4 95

TIGER WILLIAMS: WELCOME TO THE NHL, BEHN 99

RITUALS 101

TRAINERS, THE GAME'S UNSUNG HEROES 103

DEEP THOUGHTS 5 105

MY OWN TEAMMATE INJURED ME—WHAT THE FUCK! 109

MY SHOUT-OUTS TO JIMMY WATSON AND TERRY MURRAY 111

COACH BOB "CAGEY" MCCAMMON 115

DEEP THOUGHTS 6 119

LEARNING A NEW POSITION IN FIVE SECONDS 121

OUR HISTORIC UNBEATEN STREAK 125

DEEP THOUGHTS 7 127

MY SHOUT-OUT TO WILLI PLETT, WHO SHORTENED MY CAREER 133

INCHES FROM THE HOLY GRAIL BUT STILL GUTTED 137

VOTED TO THE ALL-STAR GAME 141

DEEP THOUGHTS 8 145

BACK-TO-BACK FIGHTS IN CHICAGO 147

DEEP THOUGHTS 9 149

MY SHOUT-OUT TO TIM KERR AND THE DAY I WRESTLED WITH SUPERMAN 169

DEEP THOUGHTS 10 173

MIKE BOSSY FIGHT: WHAT WAS I THINKING? 175

MY SHOUT-OUT TO KEVIN MCCARTHY 179

DEEP THOUGHTS 11 181

THE HARDEST HIT OF MY CAREER 185

PAUL BAXTER: I NEVER LEARNED TO LIKE BEING SUCKER PUNCHED 187

MY SHOUT-OUT TO MEL BRIDGMAN, THE FLEX MAN 191

THE DAY I TAUNTED WAYNE BABYCH 193

MY SHOUT-OUT TO CLARK GILLIES 195

DEEP THOUGHTS 12 199

MY SHOUT-OUT TO MARK HOWE: THE HUMBLE SUPERSTAR 203

MY SHOUT-OUT TO BARRY BECK.................................207

DEEP THOUGHTS 13 209

RANDY HOLT: GIVE ME A BREAK.................................213

KEITH MAGNUSON: CAN YOU BE SORRY YOU WON A FIGHT? 215

DEEP THOUGHTS 14 217

ARCHIE HENDERSON: WTF! 219

MY SHOUT-OUT TO BRYAN TROTTIER 223

DINO CICCARELLI: BACKCHECKING? I DON'T NEED NO BACKCHECKING.................................225

JOHN HILWORTH: A PUNCH FROM THE PARKING LOT.................................227

ADIOS AMIGOS 229

PART 4: PLAYING FOR THE CHICAGO BLACKHAWKS

MY SHOUT-OUT TO KEITH BROWN: MY ALL-TIME HERO.................................233

CONCUSSIONS ARE GOOD LUCK 235

DEEP THOUGHTS 15 241

MY SHOUT-OUT TO DENIS SAVARD 243

A GAME AND A BRAWL AGAINST TORONTO 245

MY SHOUT-OUT TO STEVE LARMER 249

RITUALS REDUX 251

THE SECOND-HARDEST BLOW OF MY CAREER 255

MY SHOUT-OUTS TO TROY MURRAY, EDDIE OLCZYK, AND CURT FRASER 257

BOB PULFORD, A.K.A. DR. BOB 261

DAVID LETTERMAN RECOGNIZES MY GENIUS AND GIVES ME FIFTEEN SECONDS OF FAME ..265

MY BACK INJURY 267

DEEP THOUGHTS 16 273

BOB PROBERT: WHY DIDN'T HE KICK MY ASS? 279

FACE SHIELDS AND THE BULLSHIT OF UNWRITTEN RULES 283

DEEP THOUGHTS 17 285

GLORY BE: WE FINALLY HAVE A RATING SYSTEM 287

SMOKING IS FUN! 291

MY SHOUT-OUTS TO MARIO LEMIEUX AND WAYNE GRETZKY 295

PART 5: FINALLY SAYING NO

A TOUGH DECISION 299

ACKNOWLEDGMENTS 305

OPENING PUNCHES

WHY THIS BOOK AND WHY NOW

1989. MY LAST YEAR IN THE NHL. TWO MONTHS LEFT IN THE season. I missed the previous year due to a broken back. The fracture had healed, but I lacked my old power.

We were playing the Detroit Red Wings. For some reason still unknown to anyone, including me, I decided it would be a good idea to run over Steve Yzerman unnecessarily hard. Once I did that, I knew Bob Probert, who was on the ice to defend his players, would immediately come after me, and we would get into a fight.

Probert was a tremendous fighter, one of the best of all time. He could have been a younger version of me. If anyone was going to knock me senseless, it was going to be Bob.

A bad back. A younger me ready to pound my face. Two months before retirement. A smart man would have just cruised out the last two months. But not me. There I was, basically asking not to get out of a ten-year NHL career in one piece.

What the fuck was I thinking? The better question is: was I even thinking at all? And the answer is no. I didn't have it in me to cruise it out. For me, this *was* the game and the only way it was played.

I played professional hockey in the NHL for ten years back in the 1980s, when the game was so violent they allowed illegal and dangerous practices to routinely go unpunished. Fans loved the fights and clamored for more—and the league was only too happy to oblige. Teams got into an arms race where they recruited tough guys—fighters—who were put on the ice to intimidate their opponents with fists, sticks, and brutal hits. And get pummeled right back. Simply put, their job was to deliver and receive hits.

Was I one of those guys? It sure looked that way. Even my own teammates thought I was getting my skull battered whenever I got into a fight.

But here's the secret of fighting in hockey: if you want to have a long career as a fighter, you have to follow three rules. Rule number one: don't get hit. Rule number two: don't get hit. And rule number three: don't get hit.

You simply can't let yourself get punched in the head. Not too often, and not too hard. If you let that happen—if you regularly got a fist to your face, nose, mouth, or skull—you wouldn't last a season, let alone a decade like I did.

Whenever I got into a fight, my first priority was to not get hit. My entire approach to fighting centered on this. I never tried to throw a punch until I could neutralize my opponent's punching arm. I did this by grabbing his uniform at the elbow with my left hand and holding on for all I was worth. After that, it may have looked like the guy was connecting, but they would be weak hits, nothing that would cause me injury.

I'll have more to say about this technique later in the book, but the point is, when I got hold of a guy in that manner, there was no way he was going to connect with power. I then had free rein to punch him hard with my right fist.

I had other skills besides fighting. I was a good defenseman. I could skate, pass, and play, and I scored over one hundred goals during my career, which is not bad for a defenseman. Even so, I'm willing to bet all the trophies I never won that most of you reading this, if you remember me at all, will remember me as a fighter. That's fair. I got into a lot of fights. That's a lot of the way the game was played back then.

When I left hockey, I left it. I did not coach, did not mentor, did no broadcasting, and stayed away from signings and nostalgia events. I didn't watch it on TV. For over thirty years, hockey was no longer a part of my life. If a business colleague or an acquaintance asked, I would tell a story or two, but otherwise hockey was firmly in the past.

One thing I *did* keep from my hockey career was all my teeth. How did I manage that? I kept my stick up nice and high.

Then, a couple of years ago, my daughter, Kristie, met a reporter named Scoop Malinowski. Scoop is always looking for stories on sports figures, and when he found out Kristie was my daughter, he asked, "You think I can get your dad to do an interview with me? I would only take up five or ten minutes of his time."

Scoop knew I hadn't done an interview since I left the game all those decades ago, and I guess he was looking for a scoop, which is pretty fitting considering his name.

Kristie thought it would be a good idea, so she told me Scoop wanted to talk to me.

"Not interested," I said.

"Dad," she said, "don't tell me you can't survive ten minutes of questions from a guy who *wants* to talk to you."

I had survived dozens of fights during my career, so she had a point. What could I say? She was pretty convincing, and I figured I could be a big boy for ten minutes. So I agreed to talk to Scoop. He asked me five questions. It was all remarkably painless—I suffered no broken bones and needed no stitches afterward—and I actually enjoyed it.

After the interview, Scoop and I talked about the current world of hockey and what some of the old guys were up to. Scoop knew a lot about a lot of players. I loved hearing those stories. It was great to think about some of those old players again and relive some memories of my own playing days.

Scoop put my interview into a book along with a whole lot of interviews with guys who played with or against me back in the day. That book was called *Facing Behn Wilson*, and I loved reading it. It was a kick seeing what the guys had to say about me. It prompted me to reach out to some of them and reconnect, and we've renewed our friendships. All thanks to Scoop getting Kristie to bug me about my hockey days. You never know how things will work out.

Once the book got published, a lot of fans got interested in me and my career, and I told Scoop I would not be opposed to getting him extra exposure. He set me up with a few podcasts where the hosts grilled me about my playing days and my fights and so on. All the aspects of my hockey life that I had not thought about in forever.

The funny thing is, once I started talking, it all came back to me. The good times, the bad times, the crazy shit that happened. It was all there.

I was no superstar, but I was a good, solid player, and I had a good career. I have a unique perspective, my own, and I started writing down some of what happened in those long-gone days. How the game was played back then. The great guys I played with and the great fighters I took on.

So here is the story of my hockey life, from when I put on my first pair of skates before I could walk to the last day close to thirty years later.

I will tell the story of my career as well and honestly as I can remember it, gloves off, good stuff and bad. Along the way, I will give some of my deep thoughts about various aspects of the game as I played it and I will also offer shoutouts to some of the amazing players I knew at that time. There will be no test at the end of the book, so please, just try to enjoy it.

My hockey years are from an era now long past, but judging from the number of comments I get when I do a podcast, they are far from forgotten. I hope some of my old teammates will read this book and remember me and get in touch. That would be great.

I think even my kids will be surprised, as they haven't heard many of these stories.

But most of all, this book is for the fans who still hold that bygone era in their hearts. I had no idea there were so many who still remembered me and my years in hockey. I hope this brings back great memories for them and they can relive some of the old days and have a little bit of fun reading about one guy's career in an unforgiving and glorious sport.

I STARTED OFF AS A YOUNG CHILD

MY HOCKEY HEROES

LET'S GET ONE THING STRAIGHT FROM THE START. IF YOU'RE looking for tales of a tortured childhood in a rough neighborhood with terrible parents, you're out of luck. This is not that story.

I was born and grew up in the suburbs of Toronto, Canada, about as safe a place as you could imagine. I had loving and devoted parents who only wanted the best for us kids and worked hard to give us a good life. My father taught high school, and my mother took care of us and the household as a stay-at-home mom.

If you know anything about Canada, you know hockey is more or less its national religion. Every kid I knew, including me, was devoted to the game and attended services as often as possible, either by playing or by watching the game.

I was one year old the first time I skated. Just shy of my second birthday. I saw my older brother skating on the rink my father built, and I screamed to my parents that I wanted to be out there on the ice with John, who was two years older than me. The problem was, no one sold skates that small, and my parents weren't about to pay for skates for someone who could barely walk. Still, to appease my screaming, they somehow put me in a pair of my mother's skates, and I went out there on the ice.

I can't now imagine how that was possible, but that's the story I was told. As I grew up, I got skates of my own, along with a stick, and I played hockey every chance I got.

We used to play street hockey in our neighborhood, just a bunch of us getting together and slapping the puck or tennis ball around. We also played on ice and in leagues. To put it simply, we played a *lot* of hockey.

Besides my older brother, John, I had a younger brother, Bart, and a sister, Laura, who was the youngest. All four of us played sports, and we were all supported 100 percent by our parents.

I can't emphasize enough how devoted my parents were to us. Besides the basics of making sure we had a roof over our heads and healthy meals to eat every day, they helped us with our homework and encouraged us in many extracurricular activities. My siblings and I were involved with all kinds of sports, but also music lessons, acting lessons, art lessons, and just about anything else our parents could dream up and afford.

Not that I was some kind of wiz kid at all this stuff. I don't think I'm technically tone deaf, but I'm about as close as you can get and I can't carry a tune. As far as art goes, don't ask me to draw anything because if I did, you wouldn't recognize it as anything other than incoherent scribbles.

My mother had gifts in both music and art, so she must have been shocked—and maybe a little disappointed—to see I inherited none of that from her.

Sports, on the other hand, seemed to be made for my brothers and me. We played whatever was in season. Indoor lacrosse in the summer, hockey (of course), basketball, track and field, baseball, soccer, and volleyball. The boys in our family were big and fast and practiced hard. All of us were good at all sports and thrived on the competition.

Surprisingly, given my eventual career in the game, my best sport was not hockey, at least compared to other players. Hockey was very competitive, even in grade school and high school, because just about every kid I knew played it. That meant I was competing against all the other kids in the school and in Toronto. It's tough to be the best under those circumstances.

We played sports every day. I always had good practicing partners in my brothers, who were always willing to play with me. Looking back, it feels like we played almost nonstop. Funny thing, the more we practiced, the better we got.

I did not have any idea of a future in the game. We just played for fun. It was my father who helped me see the value of hard work. My father was not that interested in whether we won our games or not. What he emphasized was that we had to compete and contribute. No matter what, we had to do our best and work hard for the team.

That's all he ever asked of us, and that attitude felt very supportive. It was very much an attitude that let us know he was on our side. After games we talked about how we did, where we excelled, where we fell short. When we identified some lack in our skills, he had us work on those deficiencies so we would not make those mistakes or fall behind in the same way again. He did it all in an extremely positive way.

You could say that my father was my first hockey hero. He taught me the value of hard work and what it took to contribute and be an asset to a team.

I had other heroes, of course. From the age of six or seven, I collected hockey cards with portraits and stats of my favorite National Hockey League players. We played games where we shot the cards like little flying saucers to score points. We did this at lunch, during recess, and after school. I knew a lot of the names of NHL players from those cards.

I was also playing in leagues when I was quite young. I remember one time when I was seven years old playing my first year in a league in Toronto. Coaches were serious about winning. Several times I came off a shift, and as I sat on the bench, the coach came up to me and held a piece of paper close to my face.

"Do you know what this is?" he screamed at me.

I shook my head, not understanding why this guy was yelling at me.

"It's your release papers. One more shift like you just had, and I'm gonna sign it and cut you from the team. Got it?"

Very helpful.

Looking back, I question whether that was the right thing to say to a seven-year-old, but that's how the culture of hockey was back then. Coaches could be cruel. Most were great, but some of them were just cruel. And in that league they were unpaid volunteers doing the best they could and most likely treating players exactly the way they were treated when they were young.

Today we see that kind of behaviour as abuse. It was abuse back then, too, but people didn't see it that way at the time.

The problem with yelling at a kid, besides that it's cruel, is that it doesn't work. Instead of motivating me, that kind of thing just paralyzed me. I was afraid that if I didn't go out and play perfectly, I was going to get cut. And perfection, at any age, isn't a viable goal. You do your best and you work hard, but you don't expect to achieve perfection.

About that age, I started to watch NHL games on TV. *Hockey Night in Canada* came on every Saturday and featured either the Toronto Maple Leafs or the Montreal Canadiens, and sometimes both if the schedule had them playing each other that night. Those were the only two Canadian teams at that time. I was a Toronto kid, so of course I rooted for the Leafs, but I would also watch when Montreal played. It was just magical to see pros on TV. Bigger than life!

At first, when we were still young, we were only allowed to watch the first period, and then we had to go to bed. My brothers and I complained about this. We complained about it *every* Saturday. We begged our parents to let us watch the whole game, but it was no dice at that age.

We hated it, but that was the way it was. Even though I didn't see the ends of those games, just being able to watch an NHL game was incredible to my brothers and me.

"You guys going to become pro and play for the Leafs?" my dad would ask.

"Yeah," I'd say, not realizing that it was more than just an out-of-reach dream. I had no serious thoughts in that direction at that time. I never thought I would be a professional hockey player. I was just playing along with my dad.

I admired all the greats of that era: Gordie Howe, Bobby Orr, Dave Keon, Jean Beliveau, and so many others, but my all-time favorite player when I was a little older was Denis Potvin. He eventually played for the New York Islanders, but when I saw him, he played for the Ottawa 67s, a junior team. My father took me to see him play a game against Toronto when the 67s were in town.

Potvin was phenomenal. He controlled the game from start to finish. When he was on the ice, everything worked. He moved the puck, made great passes, skated hard, worked the corners, and was just way ahead of everyone else on the rink. He made the air electric. I was in awe that someone could be that good. Watching him live made me see just how good a hockey player could be. Later, I played against Potvin for my entire professional career.

But getting the opportunity to see Potvin play wasn't even the greatest thing my dad did for me or my career. He also operated our own private hockey rink.

MY OWN PERSONAL ICE RINK

FIRST RULE OF HOCKEY: YOU NEED ICE TO SKATE ON. YOU CAN create a rink indoors just about anywhere. We had lots of indoor rinks where we grew up, but getting ice time was not easy.

That was where my father stepped in. From the time I was born, my father had a ritual every winter.

He waited until a good few inches of snow had accumulated on the ground. Then he went out and walked, baby step by baby step, to tamp it down to a thinner and denser layer. This took a while, but when he had tamped down a good section of the yard, he sprayed water on it.

This was a delicate process that could take a whole week to complete. He couldn't just let loose with a strong flow; that would just put a hole in the snow. He made as light a mist as he could with the sprayer and created a thin layer of water on the compacted snow and let it freeze. Then he added another thin layer to that. He repeated this process many times until he got a good thick layer of ice that could support us kids and our skates.

Once the rink was done, he put up a floodlight so we could use the rink after dark. In that part of the world, sunset comes pretty early in the winter. Building a rink like this was not a common thing. We were the only house in the neighborhood that had a rink in our backyard. And we had it year after year.

When it snowed, he shoveled the accumulation off the ice. As the season progressed, snowbanks grew up around the perimeter of the rink. Often, as we played, pucks went into the snowbanks and we dug around in the snow, trying to retrieve them. Sometimes we found them, but not always. When the snow melted in the spring, we often found twenty or thirty pucks there.

Sometimes our shots went over the bank and broke windows in our house. Dad never gave us a hard time about it. He just fixed the window, and we just kept playing.

We played hockey after school in our backyard, and all the neighborhood kids would come over. Eventually, my mother would call us in for dinner, and we would come in and take our skates off. Our feet would be frozen, and we would cry for about five minutes and then have dinner. After dinner, we would go back out and play. Shockingly, when we came in for bed, we would take our skates off and cry again. We played and cried twice on weekdays and three times on weekends. We seemed to be genuinely surprised that our feet were frozen each time.

My father's rink was a wonderful space for my brothers and me, and for the other kids in our neighborhood. We had amazing times on his rinks. I can still feel the snow as it sometimes fell while we were playing and hear the sounds of our skates and sticks on homemade ice that was hollow in parts. And we never had to deal with bullies.

This was not true in other parts of our lives.

DEFENDING AGAINST BULLIES

I MENTIONED EARLIER THAT I DID NOT GROW UP IN ANY KIND of rough town. While this is true, we did have bullies in our school and our neighborhood. Not that we were unique that way. Bullies are everywhere.

Where I grew up, the bullies were older kids who would see some younger kids playing basketball or baseball or some other game, and then, just because they felt like it and they were bigger, they would take the ball away and ruin the game. It must have felt pretty damn special to bully a third grader when you were in sixth grade.

Some of the kids getting bullied were my friends. Some were just my classmates. It didn't matter. I hated that the bullies thought they could do whatever they wanted to these kids, and I decided I was going to fight them.

I cannot tell you where this came from. My parents taught us right from wrong, but they sure never taught us that fighting was the way to solve problems. Nevertheless, I knew that bullies were in the wrong and whenever they did things against younger kids, it really got me mad. So mad I had to do something about it. I was a little kid. What was I thinking? Maybe this was the first instance of "gloves off"?

I remember one time I was in third grade playing soccer with other third graders. This sixth grader came along and snatched up the ball and would not give it back to us. He stood next to the grass where we were playing and held the ball on his hip, and he had this smirk on his face.

I went right up to him and told him to give the ball back.

"Make me," he said.

So I went after him. With fists high, I went in swinging. I didn't do too well in that fight, if you could call it a fight at all. He was about eleven years old, while I was about eight. He put me down pretty easily, and I ended up crying on the grass while he kept the ball.

Even though I lost that fight, it didn't stop me from taking on these jerks. Any time I saw bully behavior, I went after the bully. Most of the time I lost. They were all much older than me. I was just standing up for what was right and getting beaten up a lot for my trouble. Whether I won the fight or lost it, whether I got a bloody nose or not, I almost always cried after. I guess it was some kind of emotional release or the expenditure of leftover adrenaline. Crying was inevitable, whether I had won or lost.

My crying turned out to be a good thing, although I didn't realize it at the time. After a fight, when the teachers came out to see what was going on in the school yard and figure out how to assess some punishment, they saw a sixth grade kid standing next to a crying third grade kid and decided the older kid had to be in the wrong because no third grader would be dumb enough to go fight a sixth grader. As a result, I don't remember ever getting in any trouble for starting a fight.

I told my parents about these fights. Neither my mom nor my dad was ever angry at me about this or yelled at me about my fighting. They knew I wasn't the bully. They figured this was who I was: a guy who would protect his teammates, little kids who couldn't fight against the older kids.

I didn't understand it at the time, but my mother bought me a poster and put it up in my bedroom. It showed a vulture sitting on a branch and staring out at the viewer with a tough, menacing look. Underneath the vulture were these words: "Patience, *hell*. I'm going to go kill something."

That poster hung in my bedroom for years. I still have it today. This was just who I was, and both my parents knew it.

I'm sure they thought my fighting was just some phase or something that I would soon outgrow. I think it's safe to say they were wrong about that.

JUNIOR HOCKEY: SHIT JUST GOT REAL

AT FIFTEEN YEARS OLD, SHIT *REALLY* GOT REAL

AS MY BROTHERS AND I WERE GETTING TO HIGH SCHOOL AGE, my father figured we could translate our sports ability into a summer gig playing indoor box lacrosse in a professional league. I think he figured it would be a fun job and pay our way through college.

The three of us started amping up our lacrosse practice and playing lacrosse as hard as we could. It was great fun, and it was all going just fine until—surprise!—the league folded, and just like that our lacrosse future was over. So under my dad's direction, we pivoted to hockey.

"Hockey could be a way to jump-start your wage-earning potential," he told us one day. "You could make a lot more money in hockey than I make teaching. Let's try this and see how it goes." From my dad's perspective, we could find out if we were going to make the pros while we were young. If it didn't work out, there was still time to go back to school.

That was when shit got serious.

When I was fifteen years old, my brothers and I threw ourselves into hockey practically full time. We practiced during the summer as well, which wasn't really done back then. We found a rink where we could go play all day for $2.50. We skated and practiced and played hockey for six hours a day, five days a week.

My father believed we had a shot at professional hockey. I don't remember what I thought about that. Did I think I could make it? I didn't know. All I knew was that my father thought if I really practiced and worked hard, I *could* be a hockey success. So I practiced and worked hard. All three of us did.

And it was brutal. We drove one hour to the hockey rink, skated and trained for six hours, then drove an hour back. We came home exhausted every day, flopped down wherever we could, and fell asleep. We'd wake up in time for dinner and go to bed at seven so we would be ready for the next day, when we would go back and do six more hours of hard practice and hard skating. We did this over and over.

When I was fifteen, my brother, John, and I went to school half days, then cut class to skate every afternoon. When I was sixteen, we played junior hockey in Ottawa, and there we didn't attend school at all. We skated for four hours on our own, then did the regular team practice for two hours. I found practice to be extremely difficult—we were worn out from four hours of skating, then tried to compete at practice where most of the others were already better players and better skaters than us, and they were fresh. All that skating was to develop our speed, agility, and puck handling. We did countless sprints. It was to make us good enough to become professional hockey players.

It was a very lonely time for me. I missed my family terribly. They were almost always on my mind.

Looking back, it's almost terrifying what we did. We seemed to be skating longer than anyone else, desperately trying to catch up, yet the better players remained better. Slowly, but surely, our skating skills improved. But without that extra training, I would have never gotten into professional hockey. We built ourselves up both mentally and physically. Many other players were simply built better for the game. For whatever reason, they were also just better skaters.

I was built for running sports like lacrosse or football, where my sprinting ability could pay off, but in Canada at that time, hockey was pretty much the only option for any kind of professional sports career. I had to try to get my hockey skills up to the level of the best hockey players. That meant putting more time in than the others, which was very tough. All the other future pros were working hard in their own way. We all had to find the personal secret sauce that worked for each of us.

We played minor hockey, which is a step below Junior A. Many players in minor hockey aspired to play junior hockey. That was the step just before the NHL. You pretty much had to play junior hockey in order to have a shot at the NHL.

The thing is, you didn't go to a junior team and tell them you wanted to play for them. Scouts from the junior teams would come out and watch us play. We never knew who they were. They were just part of the audience.

This all led up to a draft into Junior A. I was drafted in the second round by the Ottawa 67s. I was sixteen years old. I had no real idea what I was getting into. But this was something I had been working toward for years. I would be required to move away from home at sixteen years old.

My choice was to be owned by the Ottawa 67s or to say no. If I refused the draft, my NHL aspirations would be effectively over. Did I really have a choice? I don't think so. *No* was never an option, and *yes* became the only answer.

I remember my brother and I packing up our VW in our driveway to go try out for the Ottawa 67s. My father helped me pack. John, who had been drafted by the same team a year before me, had some experience in junior hockey.

The last thing I remember my father saying before we drove away was to John. "Make sure you look after your brother and protect him," he said.

John was big, powerful, and brutally tough. And up to that time, I had never been in a fight on ice.

"I will, Dad," said my brother.

Then it was goodbye to my father and mother and hello to the next part of my life.

MOVING UP THE RANKS

I WAS DRAFTED IN THE SECOND ROUND. GREAT! GOOD NEWS, right? I was on the team. Nope!

Getting drafted didn't mean I was now going to get to play hockey on a junior team. All it meant was that I was going to get to compete in tryouts at training camp, just one of a hundred players, all trying to make the team. We were all more than a little anxious.

A junior hockey player in the late 1970s made $20 a week. The team covered our travel, boarding, sticks, and equipment, but still. Twenty dollars? Seriously?

That salary had been in place for a long time, probably at least thirty or forty years. No one questioned it because no one made junior hockey a lifelong career. At the most you were there for three years.

A junior hockey team has twenty players total, and when I got drafted, the Ottawa 67s had fifteen returning players from the year before. Out of a hundred hopefuls at training camp, only five were going to make the team. That meant I had only a 5 percent chance of becoming a 67er.

I knew I had to stand out, which was not easy. We were all doing what we could to stand out. There were lots of good players there. Clearly the returning players were better than the rest of us. Everyone was using their superpowers trying to make the team. I was just a sixteen-year-old kid. How was I going to let the team know I was as good as or better than any of them? How could I stand out?

The truth is, I felt desperate. I would have done whatever I had to do to make the team. I skated my best. I passed my best. I stick-handled my best. I hit my best.

I was out there hitting as hard as I could, and I was sure I was starting to make an impression. I mean, I was fearless, taking on everyone. I needed to get noticed. That was all.

I ended up pushing one guy too much or hitting him too hard. I figured I was just playing the game like I needed to play it. I was just trying to get on the team.

Maybe I made him look bad; maybe my hit hurt him. Could be anything. Who the fuck knows after forty years? All I know is in a split second we were in a fight, and it was not some schoolyard scuffle.

Gloves off, fists clenched, punches thrown.

This was my first fight in hockey, and it was a confusing experience. It felt like there were a hundred fists flying around, and they just kept flying. Some of the fists were mine, and some of them were the other guy's. I couldn't always tell whose were whose. I hadn't yet developed my fighting technique, and I didn't know how to protect myself. He took punches, and I took punches. It was chaos.

It sounds crazy, but in the heat of the moment, it felt almost like our fists were not even attached to our bodies. They were like these weapons separate from us, doing their own thing.

Eventually we got pulled apart. My uniform was ripped and twisted—a wreck. I was breathing so hard I thought I might pass out. Fighting is exhausting. It sure as hell took a lot out of me. I was actually happy to get sent to the penalty box after that fight so I could rest. I welcomed that rest in the penalty box for every subsequent fight in my career.

As I sat there with my stick beside me and my adrenaline still going like crazy, I wondered: did I win that fight, or did I get the shit beaten out of me? I had no idea.

Then I wondered: was I cut? Was my nose broken? Did I have blood all over me? I was so amped up I couldn't tell at first.

Was I in pain? If I was, the adrenaline was hiding it from me. I didn't want anyone there to think I was worried about my physical status, figuring that might make me look weak to the coach and manager, so I slowly and casually put my hand to my face just to see if there was blood.

After a little bit, I determined that I was covered in sweat, not blood, and my nose wasn't broken. And I wasn't in any pain. Fantastic! Maybe I did win that fight after all. My first fight in hockey. What a milestone!

And then another thought hit me. If I wasn't sure if I won the fight or not, maybe the other guy didn't know either. Maybe he was in just as much doubt as I was. Hell, maybe he thought he had won the fight and that he now owned my ass! That felt like an epiphany, which gave me an idea.

Right after I got out of the penalty box, I went after the same guy I just fought. I was going to show him and the whole team I was the boss. I was going to send a message. I pounded on him, and for the first time I realized I could win a fight.

By going after this guy so soon after our first fight, I made myself stand out. I showed I would do what I had to do to get on the team. It was brutal. It was nuts. But it was the way it was. I did what I had to do.

Did the coaches notice? They had to have noticed. If there were fifty fights during three weeks of training camp, I bet I was in forty-five of them.

I made the team.

HAZING IN KALAMAZOO

WHEN YOU SAY MINOR PRO HOCKEY, IT FEELS LIKE YOU'RE talking about a pretty laid-back kind of activity. Don't let the name fool you. Back then, minor league hockey was crazy!

Fans would take swings at you if they felt like it, and you were within arm's reach. They'd throw shit at you. You had to duck sometimes just to not get beaned with a beer can or something worse. Players would go into the stands and fight with fans. Like I said, crazyinsane.

I had been on the team for just a couple of months and had escaped the hazing ritual, but that couldn't last forever. One day after a practice in Kalamazoo, I had taken off my equipment and uniform and was getting ready to take a shower before putting on my street clothes, when several guys grabbed me by the arms, put me down on the floor, and held me there.

Then another guy spread a big wad of black skate polish all over my lower parts. I guess they thought that was a funny thing to do. Hazing has a long history among teams and in schools, and I don't want to get into the rightness or wrongness of it here. I kind of understood the humorous aspect of it as far as they were concerned.

But, and I mean a *big* but, the skate polish burned like hell. My balls felt like they were on fire. The pain was brutal. The guys couldn't have known it was going to burn me like that, but that didn't help me at all in this situation.

I spent the next four or five long hours in pain in the shower just trying to wash the stuff off. And it wouldn't come off. It clung to me like Velcro on glue. I turned the water to its coldest setting just to try to relieve the burning.

The rest of the team went home. I stayed behind, still trying to get the skate polish off me. The trainer couldn't leave while a player was still in the dressing room, so he had to hang around with me until I was ready to go home.

It wasn't a fun time, but there was more to come. Management got wind of me and the trainer staying long after we should have left. Maybe the trainer told them what happened. I don't know for sure, but the coach ended up yelling at the players for what they did to me.

I did not tell management anything. I knew the code: you don't squeal on your teammates. And I did not.

It didn't matter. My teammates thought I told, and they were pissed at me. It made for some awkward times in the dressing room. That's for sure.

Maybe hazing has its place, and maybe it doesn't. I will say that for me, that time in Kalamazoo, I could have done without it.

IS JUNIOR HOCKEY A REAL CAREER?

IN A WORD: NO. HOW COULD IT BE? WE WERE BROKE AND LIVING away from home. The whole point of playing junior was to get good and get noticed by an NHL team that would draft you to play for them.

For my brothers and me, the plan was to try junior hockey for a while. If it didn't work out, then we would go back to school—we would still be young enough—and learn a profession.

For my two brothers, hockey did not work out. They never played in the NHL. But for them, I think that was better in the long run. My older brother studied medicine and became a retina surgeon. My younger brother became a successful dentist.

In junior, my brother and I worked on building up our skills, still trying to catch up to the better players. The team practiced two hours every day, and John and I practiced an additional four hours a day before the team practice. We skated hard and developed our shooting and passing.

I didn't play much my first year, so I just concentrated on improving. The second and third years in junior were much better for me. I started getting a lot of ice time and some good experience playing against other teams. I was selected to play for Team Ontario in a tournament against the Russians, where I did well. I had just turned eighteen years old. I felt like I was actually a good player, and I thought I had a realistic chance of graduating from junior to the NHL.

After junior hockey, at nineteen or twenty years old, everyone has to make a decision (if you are not going to start off in the NHL). *Should I play in the minors? For how long?* There are no definitive answers to these questions. Every player has to decide for themselves. My brother John decided to go back to school. My brother Bart played one year in the minors and then went back to school. My decision proved to be easier, as I avoided the minors and went straight to the NHL.

I also played one game against my brother Bart when he was called up for the New York Rangers. He played pretty well. I was awful. All I could focus on was watching my brother play and praying he did well. Hell, if the opportunity was right, I might have passed him the puck and let him score on us. Thank god that particular opportunity didn't come up.

ROOM AND BOARD AND OLD CARS

I BOARDED WITH SEVERAL FAMILIES DURING MY JUNIOR CAREER. Most of our hosts were hockey fans who liked having a hockey player in the house. All the families were very nice and treated us well. A few times both John and I were boarded in the same house. There was always a meal when we got back from practice, so that was great. We especially liked one house where there was usually roast beef, potatoes, and a salad with thousand island dressing.

That was nice, but I vividly remember the time when John discovered a large unrefrigerated jar of thousand island dressing with a big layer of mold around the top of it, right under the lid.

John figured the host scraped off the mold and threw it away, then scooped out some of the thousand island for our salad.

That was a little bit upsetting, to say the least. Then we found out the roast beef she fed us every night was always on the kitchen counter. It never went into the fridge.

Every time I think of that, I can't help but relive my first thoughts of our little discovery. How we racked our brains trying to remember exactly how many times we had eaten salad with thousand dressing. How many roast beef dinners had we eaten?

As you can imagine, after those two discoveries, eating there was no longer appealing or even an option. We used our salaries to eat out. It took some careful planning and budgeting to eat on $20 a week, less gas money. The trick was to not spend it all in one place.

Ottawa was a very cold city in the winter. So cold that people had block heaters in their cars and heaters on their batteries. If you didn't, you wouldn't be able to get your car to start because it would be frozen. You would just crank the engine over and over until the battery died. And to be fair, no one had anything resembling a new car.

Door locks froze too. I solved this problem by carrying a little bottle of lock antifreeze around in my pocket all the time. Brilliant, right? I thought so. Most guys kept their antifreeze in the glove compartment and could not get to it because the doors would be frozen. So I figured out how to get into my car no matter what the weather.

Unfortunately, my brilliant strategy had a flaw. Multiple times the cap on the bottle came off in my pocket and the contents spilled out. I smelled like antifreeze for a few weeks each time. We didn't have money for dry cleaning. I just hoped no one smoked near me.

When we had road games, we all left our cars at our hockey arena and took a bus to the other team's town. This meant our cars weren't plugged in while we were gone. Which meant our cars would not start when we returned.

Typically, we returned from a road game at between three and seven in the morning. When that happened, we used the bus to jump-start one car and get one going. Then that car would jump-start another car, and so on until all the cars were started. This process usually took a couple of hours to complete, just to get the cars ready to drive home or, for some players, directly to school.

Talk about the glamour of hockey. We were living it every day and every night.

DOUG WILSON ALMOST ENDED MY CAREER

I FIRST MET DOUG WHEN WE PLAYED JUNIOR HOCKEY TOGETHER when he was seventeen or eighteen years old. There was nothing Doug couldn't do. He skated with grace and power, handled the puck, and possessed a cannon of a slap shot, maybe the best I've ever seen.

He was a great passer and never made a mistake. Watching him play made me think of how good Denis Potvin was that time my dad took me to see him. In my opinion, Doug could have turned pro and been a star when he was eighteen years old.

Doug was also very smart. Coaches often came up with crazy new plans or schemes that had no chance of working on the ice in an actual game. I was always dumb enough to try to follow their plans, but not Doug. He ignored the bullshit and always played his way. The correct way.

Doug got drafted in the first round of the NHL draft, seventh overall, and went on to be a perennial NHL all-star. He played on Team Canada and was elected to the Hockey Hall of Fame. None of this success surprised me or anyone who knew him. We all saw how good he was.

I was just sixteen years old when he almost ruined my career. He didn't trip me, fight me, or hit me with a stick. He made it so that I hurt myself. But it was still his fault.

I yearned to have a slap shot like his, so I began to stay after practice and work on my slap shot with him. We took turns shooting at our backup goalie.

Doug blasted the puck so hard I thought injuring the goalie was inevitable. I gamely tried my shot, but I could not shoot like Doug. No matter how hard I swung my stick at the puck, Doug's shot was always much harder. I worked on hitting the puck harder, then even harder. But I never got close to Doug's power and speed.

Then one day, after whacking away at the puck in my never-ending, futile attempt to outshoot Doug, I felt a stabbing pain on the inside of my hip. I ignored it.

The next day, we practiced shooting again. Same results. Doug had a rocket for a shot, and my shot was just okay. And now my hip hurt even more. Each day we did this, I got the same result: my shot was barely improving, and the stabbing pain kept getting worse. It got to the point where skating was quite painful.

The problem, though I didn't know it then, was with my technique. I planted my front foot perpendicular to where I was shooting, instead of forward. This prevented me from fully rotating on my swing, which kept my shot weak but also forced my hip to rotate more than a hip joint was ever intended to, and I kept jamming the ball and socket together.

I should have stopped hurting myself and figured out how to shoot the puck properly. But that was not how the game was back then. We really didn't receive any instruction on proper technique for how to skate, handle the puck, pass, or shoot. Or how to stay safe. Hockey was pretty much pass/fail. If you didn't learn it on your own, you either sat the bench or didn't make the team. There was no training in how to acquire or improve skills safely and efficiently.

Eventually, I was diagnosed with a pulled groin, and the trainer did ultrasound therapy on my leg every day. It gave me absolutely no relief. The pain just kept getting more acute.

Two years later, during my last year as a junior, our trainer was still wrapping my leg in a tensor bandage for every game and practice. But the tensor didn't help either, since a tensor is for a pulled groin, which I didn't have. I had a hip joint injury. I kept playing in pain.

It got to the point where my hip was bothering me twenty-four hours a day. My junior career was going well, and I was looking at possibly being a high draft pick for an NHL team. But it was getting *very* painful to skate. Hell, it was getting very painful to even *walk*. I had a decision to make. Could I face a career in constant pain, or should I just retire?

After serious thought, I decided I was too close to realizing my hockey dream, and I stayed in the game. Whether that was a smart thing to do or not, I don't know. And no big surprise, my hip never got any better. I played my entire career with pain every second of every game. It is painful to this day. Eventually I will have to get a hip replacement.

But it is not hard to look back and think, *If I hadn't watched Doug Wilson shoot the puck so hard and been inspired to practice shooting with him, my hip could have been fine all these years!*

You might read this and think it was envy, poor technique, and lack of basic smarts that almost ended my career. Think what you want. I like to blame Doug.

DEEP THOUGHTS 1

WHAT MAKES A GREAT PLAYER?

I PLAYED HOCKEY SERIOUSLY FOR MORE THAN TWENTY YEARS, from when I was seven to when I retired at age twenty-nine. I saw a lot in that time, and I came to develop some opinions and philosophies about the art and science of the game. I'm going to offer some of those thoughts in these sections I'm calling "Deep Thoughts."

First up, here are my opinions on the factors that make a player great.

Everyone comes to the game with their own unique abilities, unique body, and unique experience. That's just the way life works. No one is exactly like anyone else.

Raw hockey ability comes down to a few skills. You have what I call breakaway speed, which is the ability to skate well and fast. You have to be able to pass, since hockey is a team sport and you can't do it all yourself. You have to be able to shoot and score. Not on every shot, obviously, but you need to be able to score at least some of the time. You have to be able to anticipate. That means knowing what the other guy might do next and knowing where the puck is going to be in the next few seconds.

Fighting, as I explain elsewhere in this book, is a whole other game within the game. We'll leave that for a later deep thought. For now, let's just look at what makes a great *hockey* player.

A player isn't all about abilities. Every player, except for a very few superstars, also has deficits, maybe very small, but skills he is not quite as good at as he is with his exceptional skills.

Knowing all this, great players learn to identify their deficits and work on them to make them better. This is so important. Being good in all but one of the skills is not enough. If you can't pass, then it doesn't matter how good a shooter or skater you are. If you don't get better at passing, you won't be in the game for long.

I sometimes explain this by using a baseball analogy. If a hitter can hit every pitch except the slider, he isn't going to be in the majors because every pitcher will soon learn this and keep throwing sliders. He will eat sliders and be out of the league very quickly.

Similarly, if everyone knows you can't pass the puck quickly and cleanly, you will always kill any offensive opportunities that your team may have.

Or consider if a forward does not have breakaway speed. Without that threat, the opposing defenseman will play the player a little closer, taking away most of his other options.

So that's the first thing. Great players work on their deficits and really try to bring them up to their other skills.

Let's not forget that hockey is a physical sport. Great players work to keep in top shape in whatever way works. Keith Brown, my defense partner in Chicago, worked out on the bicycle machine constantly. He was always in peak physical condition, always one of the best physical specimens on the ice. Keeping in shape is hard work, but great players work hard.

Great players also have a knack for making their particular skills dominant. A good example is Mike Gartner. Mike had great break-away speed, and he didn't seem to get tired. Whenever he had a chance, he would race toward the opponent's goal with the thought of maybe getting a breakaway.

Now, most of the time, it didn't happen. He didn't get the pass, or the pass never went his way, or some other thing happened. But maybe once every twenty attempts, he *did* get a breakaway and he had a great scoring chance. The thing about those other nineteen attempts is that us defensemen had to skate with him every time to make sure he didn't get a good shooting chance. This was exhausting. It exhausted me playing against him because he didn't seem to get tired. He skated at top speed from the first face-off to the last buzzer. That gave him an enormous advantage over me and most other defensemen.

He was strong on his skates and had inexhaustible speed. That was his superpower, what made him great, a Hall of Famer. Envy is not the right word to describe what I thought about Mike's skating. I certainly admired it and wished like hell I had his superpower.

Remember my earlier story about Doug Wilson and his wicked shot? The point of that story was how he fucked up my hip. But there's another side to that story.

Doug Wilson was practicing his shot. Why? He already had a fantastic, incredible shot. The reason is that great players don't rest on their abilities. They are always trying to improve, trying to get that extra edge that will give them an advantage. Doug wasn't there taking practice shots just to make my life difficult. He was there every day to get even better.

My body was a sprinter's body. I could handle myself very well in short bursts of skating, like the length of the rink. With longer lengths, where we might go up and down the ice a dozen times, I was not able to keep up with the best. This was not due to lack of conditioning. My sprinting ability was a big asset for me. I had fast twitch muscles. Endurance was another thing entirely.

I knew this early on, which was why my brother and I would skate six hours a day in junior. We were trying to build up our muscles, which were made for sprinting, to the point where they could work for us in longer distances.

I did get better. No doubt about it. I could more or less keep up with the elite skaters in sprints, but absolutely not in long distances. Thank god hockey is mostly a series of short bursts for defensemen.

One other factor that great players have is anticipation. This is an uncanny ability to see where the play is going, where the puck will be in a couple of seconds, and where they should be to take advantage of any situation. These guys, like Gretzky and Lemieux, for example, saw the play unfold and knew where to go a little faster than the rest of us. It wasn't binary. Average players anticipate better than poorer players, good players better than average, and so on. Gretzky and Lemieux just sat at the top. They had so many scoring opportunities, so many breakaway situations, even when all of us knew they were looking for breakaways.

Natural ability, great skills, fit body, and the determination to work hard. That's what makes a great hockey player.

WHO HAS TIME FOR SCHOOL?

IN CASE YOU THINK MY THREE YEARS IN JUNIOR HOCKEY WERE just wall-to-wall fun and games with me getting into brawls, trying to scrape skate polish off my privates, fucking up my hip for life, and eating moldy thousand island dressing, don't forget when I started playing for the Ottawa 67s I was still a kid. Sixteen years old. I was only partway through high school, which meant I had to figure out how to graduate if I could.

You might ask, "What's the big deal? After a game or practice, just hit the books, study hard, and pass the courses. Simple."

Not exactly. The season in junior hockey was sixty-eight games. Add ten exhibition games to that, plus playoffs, and you're talking almost the equivalent of a full NHL season. School starts at eight in the morning, and often the team bus did not get back to town from a game until five or six in the morning. It was brutally tough for the guys to get off the bus and go directly to school for classes, then right to practice after school.

Some players tried to go to school during the season and ended up missing a few days because of practice or games or just being exhausted. Then they were kicked out of high school because they missed three days, and they had to repeat that grade the next year. I saw it happen a lot, and to put it mildly, it was a no-win way to get an education.

School was important to me. I mentioned my father was a teacher. He made sure all of us did well in school, and he really instilled in us a love of learning and helped us see the importance of education. One of my brothers became a dentist, and the other practices as a retina surgeon. You don't get into those kinds of careers by not paying attention in school. As for me, my destiny was not to be in the medical profession, but I sure never wanted to be a high school dropout.

I also didn't want to lose my hockey career. What to do? I tried correspondence courses for a while and did pass one class that way, but taking correspondence courses was a tough way to go through high school. My brother and I came up with a solution. At the end of each season, we returned to our parents' house, went to our old school, and asked our teachers, the ones we knew, if they would let us study on our own.

"If we teach ourselves," we said, "can we just take the exam, and if we pass, then we pass the course?"

This was not the normal way of doing school, or even summer school, but we knew we had to cram a whole year of studying into a very short time. Our teachers knew us and liked us and agreed to our plan.

John was extremely good at math, and we studied together. I remember one year we had to learn grade thirteen calculus (equivalent to first-year college) in about three weeks. We studied eighteen hours a day, seven days a week.

There were times I looked at John and said, "I don't understand this. I don't know what we're doing."

John was big and strong and powerful, and he would grab me by the shirt and hold me close to his face and squeeze me hard. "Behn," he would say, "it doesn't matter if we understand this or not. All we gotta do is learn the right steps and pass the tests."

He was right, I guess. So we continued studying. We took a test every day or two. Often we had just learned the material on a test the night before.

After I took one of these tests, the teacher once asked me if I was ready for the next test the next day.

"Nope," I said.

"But you're going to learn it tonight?"

"Yup," I said. And we did. With John's help and with concentrated study, we passed. More than that. We made sure we made great grades in case we had to go back to school full time.

I repeated this level of intense studying three times, once after each season in junior.

It was brutal and maybe not the best education, but I did get my diploma. The upside of this way of going to school was that I did not have to do any studying during the hockey season. I could just concentrate on the games, on practice, and on trying not to get injured, which, as you will see, did not always work out for me.

PUCKS HURT

DURING MY LAST YEAR IN JUNIOR HOCKEY, I WAS EIGHTEEN, and we were on the road playing against the Sudbury Wolves. This was a good tough team, and it was a hard-hitting, hard-playing game.

They were in our end, and one of their defensemen got the puck at the blue line and was getting ready to shoot. As a defenseman, my job was to clear opposing players from the area in front of the net. So I pushed their player who was parked there out of the way. This gave our goaltender a good look at the shot that was about to come his way.

I pushed the player a good ten feet wide of the net. Plenty of room for our goalie to get a bead on the puck.

The opposing defenseman, still at the blue line, took his shot. He managed to miss the side of the net by ten feet and the top of the net by two feet. What he *did* hit, instead of the net, was me. In my head.

Somehow the puck missed my helmet and hit my temple square on. I was down on the ground in an instant. I might have been out cold. I'm still not sure if I was or not. What I do remember is when things got back into focus, I was on my hands and knees with blood pouring out of the wound and dripping onto the ice.

They took me to the dressing room, where I got stitched up and ready to go back on the ice. Except I wasn't. Not really. I had clearly sustained a concussion, and I should have been out for the game, and maybe for a few games, but that's not how things were back then.

If you got injured on the ice, you got stitched up, and you were good to go play. The team figured you were tough enough to play, and no player ever said anything different.

The drill was, when a coach or trainer asked if you were good to go, your answer was always yes. And that was the end of it.

This attitude, dangerous as it was, was drilled into me from my first days playing hockey. My father always said, "You never let anyone else take your shift."

Coming up through the little leagues, hardly any player *ever* said he couldn't play. Most would never think of saying it. You could always play. No matter what, you were ready to play. The message was as clear as it could be: never show you're hurt.

By the time I got hit with that frozen puck, this attitude was so hardwired into me that it was inconceivable that I would ask to not play in this game.

So I took my shifts for the rest of the game. I was out there on the ice even though I had little idea what I was doing. My vision was foggy. My judgment was off. I was in great pain, and I could only see out of one eye.

The game ended. I don't remember who won. We all piled into the bus and headed to Sault Ste. Marie for a game the next night.

The next morning I woke up to such swelling around my temple that it felt like a blown-up balloon, so big I couldn't even open my eye. I tried to wedge a couple of fingers between my eyelids to push them open, but that didn't work. My eye was swollen shut tighter than a frozen car door.

I looked in the mirror and saw that the puffiness was held together only by the stitches. I believe if I had so much as brushed those stitches with a napkin they would have ripped wide open.

Later that day, I was finally able to pry open my eye enough to see that my eyeball, under all that swelling, was completely bloodshot. Red as a giant cherry. This was certainly alarming, but on the plus side, I *could* see through that eye, so I was relieved that I wasn't blind. That was some consolation. But on top of the swelling, the entire area, from my temple to my eye socket, was extremely painful.

I might have had a broken bone in there somewhere. Whenever I touched it, the pain was brutal, so something was going on. It was sore to the touch for years. I probably should have gotten an X-ray or even had an ophthalmologist take a look at my eye, but we had a game that night, and I was simply not capable of saying I was too hurt to play, even with only one functioning eye.

A few hours later, just before the game, the coach saw I was pretty badly injured.

"You okay to play?" he asked.

"Yes," I said.

And that was that. I played that game with one eye.

Looking back, that was insane.

I also knew that if anyone so much as nudged me, those stitches would come undone, and my wound would rip wide open. What to do?

I came up with a plan. For the entire game, I was going to make sure I didn't get into any fights, and I was going to keep my stick up high. Not fighting would make sure my wound would not get opened up by a punch, and keeping my stick up would defend my wound from getting hit in other ways. This was not just a plan. In my mind it was the *only* plan possible.

It might be worth quoting the boxer Mike Tyson here, who once said something like "Everyone has a plan until they get punched in the face." Hold that thought while I tell you how the game unfolded.

My plan went well for a while. I could only see half the rink at any one time, as I only had one good eye, but I was managing.

Then at some point during the game, my defense partner got run over badly in our corner, so I had to go in and take out the guy that hit him. I used my stick so as not to put my injured eye in jeopardy. Some of his teammates took exception to my hit, and a couple of them came after me. My plan, as I said, was to not get in a fight, so I cross-checked the players who were trying to take me on.

It resulted in a bench clearing brawl, with all the players from both teams out on the ice, each of them pairing off with an opposing player and ready to fight. I had lost my stick, and everyone was squaring up. I lined up against Ted Nolan.

Being a good fighter meant calling up the rage that is deep down inside you and letting it come out for the fight. Some guys have the rage. Some guys don't. Some guys were fighters. Some weren't. A lot of that depended on whether they had the rage.

I had that kind of rage times ten. I knew I couldn't let Ted land a punch on my injury, so I used my rage to pound on him so hard and so quickly that he couldn't lay a finger on my eye. This was not part of any plan. It was pure instinct born of pure rage, something I almost couldn't control in that moment. It came from me having to protect my eye. I was ready to do anything I needed to do, and my rage was my best weapon.

I respected Ted. He was a scrappy guy and a real competitor. He later went on to coach the Buffalo Sabres, but that night it was just him and me, man on man, with me doing everything I could to *not* get hit.

As it turned out, I beat him pretty badly. He never laid a finger, much less a fist, on my face or eye. We ended up down on the ice, me sitting on top of him while hitting him over and over. I did everything I could to make sure my injury was protected.

After pounding on Ted for a while, with the rest of the players getting into fights and tussles all around me, I realized if Ted's teammates saw me pounding on him like I was, they would come over and jump on me. So I stopped the fight. I stopped hitting Ted, got up on my skates, and let him go.

The brawl raged around me. I felt pretty good that I had protected my eye, but then, to my complete disbelief, Ted came back for me.

I give him credit. He was beaten up pretty badly, probably had a broken nose, but he wanted a rematch. He picked the wrong guy that night. I still had the rage, and I was ready to use it as many times as I needed to. He came at me, and it was just like the first round. I hammered him badly, and once again, he didn't lay a finger on me.

We finally skated away from each other as the bigger brawl around us was breaking up. Players were collecting their gloves and sticks from the ice, all of us breathing hard and exhausted, some of us bleeding, some of us triumphant, some of us destined for the penalty box or the training room to get stitched up.

As all this unfolded, all I could think was that I had saved my eye from further injury, but all things considered, maybe it would have been better to have just taken the game off.

ALLERGIES SUCK

EVERYONE HAS ISSUES THEY NEED TO DEAL WITH. THINGS THAT might keep them from reaching their potential or that they have to try to overcome. In hockey, you could be too tall or too short, have a sore or unstable knee, or have a muscle type unsuited for hockey. It could be anything. The list is endless. I was no different.

From an early age, I've had to live with significant allergies. Pollen, dust, and mold affected my breathing. It has dogged me my entire life. Fortunately, medications, air filters, and non-allergenic beds and pillows have greatly improved over the years and now provide some welcome relief.

But before all that, I was always blowing my nose, always dealing with nasal infections. I don't think I was able to breathe through my nose for over thirty years. This greatly fatigued me, and it affected my play. Hockey arenas are cold places filled with mold. When we were on the road, hotel rooms were filled with dust. All those factors affected my breathing and energy levels.

People thought I wasn't trying hard. Coaches were always giving me a hard time about my effort. I also had a long stride, which made it look like I wasn't skating hard.

The press got into it too. There were all kinds of stories in the newspapers and sports magazines about how "Behn Wilson doesn't give good effort on the ice," how "he's a lackluster player with low energy just doing the bare minimum to get by."

All those stories were full of shit but difficult to listen to. I practiced *hard* for six hours a day every day when I was younger. I wasn't some lazy-ass player trying to coast without contributing. I was a hard-working player, in great shape, who happened to be dealing with crushing allergies all the time.

I felt it pointless or even counterproductive to confront those reporters and never brought up my allergies with the coaches. I figured if I did, I would sound like a whiner or someone full of excuses, and no one wants to hear *that* guy. I certainly didn't want to *be* that guy, so I kept my mouth shut and went out on the ice every day and fought like a motherfucker for my team. If some people thought that was low energy, well, there wasn't anything I could do about that. But it still hurt.

Early on, after I made it onto the 67s, I did wonder if I should keep going in hockey. Maybe it would have been best for me to drop out of hockey altogether and go back to school. The allergies took a lot out of me.

I'm not exactly sure why I stayed. I suppose part of it was that I didn't want to disappoint my father, who had high hopes for me having a hockey career. Also, by that time, I had invested a lot of time and effort into hockey, and it felt like a waste to walk away from it just before I had a chance at the NHL.

Everyone has an Achilles' heel. Allergies were mine. I took what life gave me, good and bad, and ran with it. I think everyone does the same.

LEARNING TO FIGHT WAS MY SUPERPOWER

FIGHTING WAS A BIG PART OF THE GAME BACK WHEN I WAS moving up the ranks to eventually get to play in the NHL. I always felt that just dropping your gloves and being willing to get into it made you a winner.

In the minor leagues, before junior, fighting was not allowed, and I was perfectly fine with that. Once I got to junior, it was completely different. In junior, fighting was definitely allowed, tolerated, and even encouraged.

I picked up on that right away and knew if I could show myself as tough and willing to fight, I could make myself valuable and make the team. After all, being able to defend your teammates and being able to intimidate the opposing team is a big plus.

Back then, there were always two games going on at once. There was the real game, the one where you had to try to keep up with the superstar goal scorers like Gretzky, Messier, and Trottier. That was tough enough. Then there was the other game, the violent game, where hits were hard and sometimes illegal, where fights happened, where intimidation ruled, where things could get ugly.

Not too many players could do the pure violent game for long. I believe for most guys it was about two years and they were out. Fighting in hockey is not like fighting in the boxing ring. There you have rules and a set amount of time for each round and so on. In hockey, you never know if someone's going to cross-check you from behind, hit you with a sucker punch, or jump you from behind and start a fight.

Then there's the true joy of a fresh player being put on the ice near the end of the game to fight with players, like me, who had been playing the whole game and were dog tired.

But some guys could play both games. These guys were rare. I think of a tremendous player like Terry O'Reilly, who played both games, the real one and the violent one, for fifteen NHL seasons and played them both exceptionally well. To me, that counts as one of the most amazing hockey feats ever.

Like many of the skills needed to play hockey, fighting was never taught. It was truly on-the-job training. You either learned to fight, learned how to punch effectively on skates and defend yourself from punches, or you were out. It was just that simple.

Strength, balance on skates, rage, and strategy are all crucial to fighting. But not letting yourself get hit hard in a fight is the real secret.

Sure, when you see players fight, it looks terrible, and sometimes it is. But for a fighter to have a long-term career, there is no way they can allow themselves to be pummeled hard by opposing players.

During my fighting years, I worked to make sure I was hit as little as possible, as weakly as possible, or not at all. In most fights, I never got hit. I didn't even try to swing a punch until I had my opponent's punching hand tied up. This meant he could swing, even swing hard, but I effectively caught the punch with my arm. It might have looked good, but the punch seldom hit my face, and if it did, there wasn't enough power in the punch to have any effect.

Personally, I rated my fights by whether I got hit or not. If I didn't get hit, that was a good fight. And if I did get hit but the hit had little power, that was also a good fight. Me hitting my opponent was not a true measure of a good fight. Getting good punches on my opponent was the *fun*.

I had a brutal fight with Curt Fraser. His punches were hard enough to hurt me badly, and I think vice versa, but we were both able to neutralize each other's power. Make no mistake: one slip-up or error, and a devastating punch would have landed on at least one of us.

The key to winning any fight is always to avoid the hard hits. The situation with Curt was extremely precarious. We were both just inches away from landing a knockout blow or being hit with a knock-out blow. Too close!

My teammates and others often commented that I could really take a punch. But my *actual* fighting superpower was hardly ever getting hit. I tolerated a limited number of hits that had no effect, like when Clark Gillies hit me. Much harder hits and scarier hits were when lefty Terry O'Reilly hit me. I had no defense against a lefty. My one hard hit that I remember was from Willi Plett. I don't know how many of those anyone could really sustain.

When I look back on that part of my career, when the fighting started and when I sustained my fighting over the years, it feels to me like I was in the right place at the right time. It was a time when rage and an instinct to protect people from bullies was valuable.

I ended up in a career that nurtured that part of me, that rewarded me for fighting. I fought to protect my teammates and intimidate my opponents. I believe in life we either nurture our best qualities or our worst qualities, and as I write these words today, I can truly say I don't know whether my fighting instinct was a good quality or a bad quality.

I just know it worked for me and for my teams. And back then, that was more than good enough.

EMPLOYED AS AN ASSASSIN

I WAS NOT A FIGHTER IN A VACUUM. I WAS NO TRENDSETTER OR influencer. It wasn't like before me hockey was a tranquil, gentle sport full of solicitous gentlemen playing a refined game, and after me hockey was a brawling free-for-all fight club. Hockey was always tough, full of checks and hits. But as I was coming up, the game was becoming more and more violent, and none of that was on account of me.

The Philadelphia Flyers in the 1970s earned the nickname the "Broad Street Bullies" because of their aggressive style of play. And when I say aggressive, I mean some went out on the ice with the singular purpose of brutalizing the other team.

Other teams didn't have the pure fighters that Philly had. None of this was fair, and none of it was right. One of my ideas for a title for this book was *What Were We Thinking?* Obviously that didn't make the final cut, but it says a lot about the culture of the game and how it was played back then.

And a lot of times it was *very* unfair. Cross-checking is a dangerous thing to do. It involves holding your stick up high with both hands and going after a player with the intention of hitting him—often in the back or head—with the stick. It inflicts significant pain (at the least), with little to no consequences to the cross-checker. Say player A cross-checks player B in the face. Player B gets a bad injury involving broken teeth or a broken cheekbone, and player A gets a two-minute penalty. I call that not just unfair but dangerously unfair.

And it wasn't all the players' fault. The league seemed to be okay with the excessive rough play. Maybe because the fans loved it. They cheered like crazy when fights broke out. If I had been consulted about the whole thing, I might have urged the hockey poobahs to find ways to cut down on the fighting. Then again, maybe not. After all, my fighting abilities made me valuable to the team. Funny thing, no one ever asked my opinion on the matter, one way or the other.

The culture of violence kind of took off and gained its own momentum. Referees gave out only minor penalties for egregious infractions and often didn't call penalties at all. Were they told to do so? I don't know. I just know we could get away with a lot. There were hundreds of times after the whistle had blown that I had two or three seconds to get in a good cross-check on a guy. I seldom got a penalty for this sort of illegal tactic.

I actually poked fun at some of our goal scorers about this. "Hey," I'd say in the dressing room, "if you guys are so smart, how come you slow down when the whistle blows? That's when you are easiest to hit and I get in a few good shots."

In any case, the Flyers went to three Stanley Cup finals in a row and won two of them. In other words, the tough tactics worked. Now don't get me wrong; they also had exceptional players in Clarke, Leach, Barber, and Parent. But the intimidation didn't hurt.

The intimidation worked so well that other teams adopted the same style in an effort to meet the threat from Philadelphia. It meant some mediocre players who did not have great hockey skills could have careers if they were good fighters and, most importantly, if they were *willing* to fight. Some very talented players lost their careers because they couldn't take the daily beatings.

It became an arms race, with each team competing for an arsenal of good enforcers. A lot of big guys came into the league back then, guys who could fight. The result was a more violent game across the board. The NHL style filtered down to junior, where fighters tried to show their aggressive side to get noticed and to get called up to the NHL. That's sure what I did. I could see the writing on the wall, and I saw what was going to work, what was going to get me a career.

In my first year in junior, we were playing an exhibition game, and I was still trying to make the team. Just before the third period, in the dressing room, the coach announced in front of everybody, "John, Behn, if you two go out and fight their two tough guys, I'll sign you to the team tonight."

We knew what two players he was talking about without him telling us. They were the toughest guys on their team, and they had been playing rough all night. They were also nineteen years old, I think, and had full beards, while I, at sixteen, only had peach fuzz. I wasn't as physically mature as those guys. It was very intimidating, but John and I were both desperate.

Shockingly, my brother John and I both got into fights that night. And—surprise!—it was with their two tough guys. Fighting older, more mature guys did wonders for my rage. Rage was my best friend. We both did well in those fights and made the team. We now were effectively assassins. Sent out to kill.

We were on the team, but we didn't play much that first year. Coach would send us out late in the game to fight. It wasn't much ice time, and just getting called to fight was a depressing way to spend the season.

We joked about how we might get more ice time.

"I bet," said John, "if we don't get into a fight the first shift, that'll force the coach into having to put us out for another shift. Double our ice time!"

We never did that, but we sure thought about it. We wanted to be out on the ice playing the game, not held in reserve as ammunition just as the game was ending.

None of what I've said here makes fighting either right or wrong. All I'm saying is that fighting was a part of the game, and no one could escape it. Unless you wanted out of hockey, you had to figure out how to get along with fighting in one way or another. You found a way to deal with it or you were out.

THE NHL DRAFT: ALL THE MARBLES IN ONE DAY

AFTER THAT FIRST YEAR I GOT A LOT MORE ICE TIME. AT THE end of my third season in junior, the draft for the NHL was held in Montreal. By that time my brother John had gone back to school, but he went with me to the draft. I was glad to have him there. He was a great support.

The draft was one of those make-or-break moments for my career. If I wasn't drafted, it meant hockey was over for me at nineteen years old.

My brother and I arrived at the hotel conference room where the draft was being held. There was a stage with a microphone behind a podium. Maybe a hundred or so players sat on chairs in the audience, all waiting for a word about their future.

Every ten minutes or so, a league representative came out on stage and said something like, "The Toronto Maple Leafs draft center forward John Doe." Then the announcer walked off the stage and didn't return for another ten minutes. John Doe would stand up to applause from the room and acknowledge with a high fist or maybe just a smile, depending on what kind of guy he was.

I wanted to be one of those John Does. I wanted to be drafted, and I wanted to be drafted in an early round because those guys were likely to make more money than guys drafted in later rounds. I'd had dinner the previous night with the Philadelphia Flyers' management. It seemed auspicious, but no guarantees.

Once a team drafts you, they own your rights. You played for them, or you didn't play. Seems unfair. You couldn't negotiate with other teams to leverage a better offer. In every other business, this is called restraint of trade, but not in sports. I didn't care. I just wanted to play pro.

The waiting was nerve-racking. My stomach was full of butterflies. I couldn't imagine being drafted outside the first round, but again, no guarantees.

Thank god I didn't have to wait too long. The announcer came out, tapped the microphone, and leaned close to it. Like the previous five announcements, everyone in the room got real quiet. Some held their breath. Some closed their eyes. I felt my heart beating fast.

The next words that came out of his mouth changed my life forever. "With the sixth pick in the first round," he said, "the Philadelphia Flyers draft defenseman Behn Wilson."

I stood up. John, next to me, also stood, grabbed my hand, and gave me the hardest handshake I've ever had along with about the biggest hug I've ever gotten. It was great having him there to share that moment with me.

He didn't have to say anything!

All that work, all that effort, all that sacrifice finally paid off. I was going to be a professional hockey player. I was going to play for the Broad Street Bullies.

PART 3

TURNING PRO IN PHILADELPHIA

I'M A FLYER——ALMOST

IN ACTUALITY, OF COURSE, THE FLYERS WERE NO LONGER thought of as the Broad Street Bullies. By the time I got there, that nickname had mostly faded away with their previous era of unrivalled toughness. The Flyers were a good team with great players and excellent chances of *making* the playoffs and doing *well* in the playoffs. That had not changed. And they were still tough.

But in 1978, when I joined the organization, all the other teams had amped up. Tough as the Flyers were, they were no longer unique. You could say every team was a bully team. That was what it took to do well in those years.

I got drafted on a Thursday and agreed to a contract on Friday. Philadelphia offered me a lot of money to play for them. At the time, it felt like all the money in the world. Half a million over four years, with $150,000 of it on signing. Truly, as a kid, I thought I was the richest guy in the world, and, funny thing, lots of people around me also thought I was the richest guy in the world. People told me I should buy a big expensive car, a nice house, and all kinds of shit I didn't need.

By Sunday, once I sat down and thought about it, I realized the math didn't work. Even if I had a long career, and that was by no means guaranteed, that money was not going to last me for the rest of my life. I would need another career, but I had never done anything other than play hockey.

So I decided right then to save as much money as I could. As my career went on, I used my summers to learn business. I interned with real estate development companies. I sat in on meetings, saw how acquisitions worked, and learned a whole lot. I also took college business courses.

As the years went by, my hockey notoriety got me meetings I wouldn't otherwise have gotten, and I learned from some very smart and successful people how to succeed in business.

In my later years, some of the guys I played with didn't get why I did all this during my off season.

"Let me ask you something," I would say. "Do you think your accountant could knock you down and take the puck from you?"

"No," was the obvious reply.

"While we were skating and training, those guys went to school to learn their profession. They took courses, studied, and gained experience in their vocation, just like us. So what makes you think you can just quit hockey and step into some other line of work without developing the skills to do it?"

No answer to that. I think I made my point.

Not that any of those considerations dampened my enthusiasm for hockey. I was ready to play for the Philadelphia Flyers and happy they wanted me.

I was in the Flyers system. Did that mean I was on the team? Nope. I still had to prove myself at training camp. By the time I was drafted to the Flyers, I could skate as well as I could walk or run. That must sound impressive. Hopefully the Flyers' management would think so as well. The only problem was that *everybody* there could skate as well as they walked or ran. Just like my first days in junior, my first days with Philadelphia involved trying out for the team with other draftees, mostly rookies like me. The returning players came a week later.

Unlike junior, I didn't need a lot of fights at the Flyers' training camp to prove I was good enough. I had one fight there. Just one. That was refreshing. Despite my reputation as an enforcer and a fighter, I was happy not to have to get into any fights. Fighting can be a huge distraction and a debilitating drain on both body and mind. As the game within the game, it requires just as much concentration and effort as hockey itself.

One thing that *was* like junior was the hazing. All the other guys liked to razz the rookies. I was cool with that. The new guy can always expect to be the butt of jokes at first.

It went a little further than that, though. I was placed in the Flyers' minor league team's dressing room for training camp. The minor league veterans made it very clear that I was in for a long year with them. I said nothing, but I wasn't planning on playing in the minor league. I was planning on making the NHL with the Flyers my first year.

While I was out on the ice one day, someone on the minor league team got into my changing stall and cut off one of the pant legs from my pants. Ha ha. Real funny. At least it wasn't skate polish to my privates. All I had to do was walk back to the hotel missing a pant leg. Who cared? I figured that was that and hoped they wouldn't cut all my clothes.

Except it was a big deal. Someone in management must have seen me walking with one covered leg and one bare leg, and they said something to the veterans of the minor league team.

To be absolutely clear, I did not say anything to management. But just as in Kalamazoo, I immediately was accused of ratting on my teammates, and no amount of me saying otherwise changed their minds. Remember, I was out in public with only one pant leg. Anyone could have seen me and said something that could have gotten back to management. But I guess the players figured there was no other way management could have known except directly from me.

So the next time I was on the ice, they decided to hide my pants completely. I wasn't about to go back to the hotel with *no* pants, so I grabbed Dave Hoyda's pants from his stall. Dave was one of the main instigators of hazing on the team, so I figured he knew where my pants were. We were about the same size, so I figured I'd wear his pants back to the hotel, and he'd wear my pants back to the hotel.

Everything would work out okay. We'd have a laugh and give each other our proper pants, and that would be the end of it.

Turns out David did *not* know where my pants were, and the guys who *did* know did not want to tell him. I don't know how Dave got to the hotel without his pants, but whatever he had to do must have really made him angry because a couple of hours later, when I was in my hotel room, I heard a knock on the door. I opened it, leaving the chain on, to see Dave and six other guys standing there looking very pissed.

"What do you guys want?" I asked.

Dave didn't answer. Instead, he kicked in the door. I stepped back. All seven of these big guys came into my room. They looked like they were ready to kill. We exchanged words. Things were very tense. I was 100 percent sure they were there to beat me up. All over some pants.

It was crazy. I thought, *Fighting my teammates in a hotel room for free is not part of the game.* They made some threats. I told them to fuck off. More threats. More words. I braced myself to get pounded. Ultimately that didn't happen. I gave Dave back his pants, and pain and bloodshed was fortunately averted.

DEEP THOUGHTS 2

WHAT MAKES A GREAT TEAM?

IT HELPS TO HAVE SUPERSTAR GOAL SCORERS. THAT IS THE KEY. No doubt about it. But to have a really great team, a team that wins playoff series and goes on to win the Stanley Cup, you absolutely must have great goaltending. Without it, a team will not go far. I can't name one Stanley Cup champion that did not have the top goalie in the league.

Great goalies do two crucial things. One, they do not let bad goals in. If you beat a great goalie, it's because you did something great, not because of any lapse on the goalie's part. Two, they make incredible saves when their team makes a mistake. If I try to take the puck out of my end and the opposing forward takes it from me with a clear shot on goal, that's my mistake. When a great goalie like Pete Peeters stops that shot, that's the goalie making sure my mistake doesn't lead to a goal.

If you have a goalie who can do those two things consistently, you have a great goalie and a chance at a great team.

Defensemen and goalies are like a tight little family. We often socialized together, and we took pride in helping each other out. Goalies loved it when I stopped a shot on goal, and I loved it when they saved a goal after one of my mistakes. If a player ever rolled over my goalie, I was right there, on the spot, rolling over him and taking the penalty. My job was to protect the goalie and I took that seriously.

When I played with the Flyers, the guys told me about Bernie Parent, who was their goaltender when they won the Stanley Cup a few years before I came on the team.

"You couldn't score on him," they said. "Even in practice, he'd be laughing and joking around with us, but you still couldn't score on him. No one could."

When we went to the finals against the New York Islanders, Pete Peeters was hot as well. It was incredibly hard to score on him, whether it was during practice or during the game. Without him, we wouldn't have gotten as far as we did.

It almost sounds too simple, but basic truths often are simple. If the guy standing in front of the net and protecting it from incoming pucks does an exceptional job, then your team has a fighting chance of doing well. Without that, you're up a creek.

Okay, we've covered one end of the ice. What about the other end? Don't you need great scorers to have a great team? Yes, you do. It's all well and good to have a goalie stopping the opposing team's shots, but you also need guys on your team who can beat the other goalie.

I call these guys goal scorers and superstars. It's no great intellectual feat to understand how goal scorers help the team. When Wayne Gretzky was on the Oilers, racking up all those millions of goals, it's no wonder Edmonton won all those cups. But there's a little more to it than that. Gretzky was on that great first line that could go up against any other line in the league. But Edmonton also had a great second line with Mark Messier. If not for Gretzky, Messier's line would have been the first line. They were that good.

So in Edmonton's top two lines, you essentially had two first lines that could play at least evenly against any other first line in the league. In other words, they had *depth*. Would Edmonton have been as great if they'd only had Gretzky and no other superstars? Nope. One superstar isn't enough. One great line isn't enough. You need a great second and even third line to be a great team.

When we were playing Edmonton back in those days, our fourth line never went up against their first or second line or vice versa. If by chance or error that happened on a shift change or some other mix-up, the mix-up often resulted in goals against us.

Their depth gave them another advantage. Edmonton's fourth line was not made of superstars or goal scorers. They could come out a few times during the game, and their job was to make trouble. Even before the puck was dropped, they would get into pushing and shoving, and then, if I was on the ice, I would have to grab them and wrestle with them for thirty seconds or a minute or so, whatever it took before the refs broke us up.

I remember one of their players, McClellan, was very good at this sort of thing. He'd tie me and my teammates up for a while. I tried not to get into any fights with him because against Edmonton, you couldn't take too many penalties. Their power plays were lethal. So instead, we'd get tired out from the pushing and shoving, and then they'd go back on the bench, and Gretzky's line, or Messier's line, fresh as clean laundry, would come out ready to roll over us.

McClellan is an interesting player because his career illustrates the difference between a great team and an ordinary team. I just described how he would hack and chip at me, for example, knowing that I wouldn't fight back too hard because I couldn't risk a penalty.

Well, one season he was traded to the Hartford Whalers, and it was a very different story between us. Without Gretzky and Messier, McClelland couldn't antagonize without consequence. He didn't give me trouble because he knew I would take a penalty against Hartford. I took it to McClelland, cross-checking, hitting, and just playing my regular game.

As bad luck would have it, however, he was traded back to Edmonton, and it was the same old shit. I really saw how a great team orchestrates its own advantage by seeing McClelland play on those two teams.

One more thing about great teams. A hockey season changes from the beginning to the end and often changes again going into the play-offs. During the first half or so, there is a lot more free skating, and the checking isn't as close. That means you need certain players who can play that game. As the season progresses, the checking gets tighter, and the games get tougher, so you need players who can handle that type of game.

Great teams have both kinds of players. A good example here is Bob Nystrom. In the first half of the season, he was there, but he was not dominant. In the second half, it was his kind of game, and he became an extremely valuable player who could hit and play tight so that you couldn't skate around him. He was in his element in those games.

The upshot is that great teams have two kinds of depth. They have great lines, and they have players who can play any kind of game, no matter where they are in the season.

Add to that great goaltending, and you have a formidable team.

A FLY ON THE WALL

MY FIRST TIME IN THE PHILADELPHIA DRESSING ROOM WAS absolutely incredible. Being with all the players there felt like an out-of-body experience. That's the only way I can describe it. I came in and saw all these great players, some of them already legends, who I remembered watching at home on television with my family.

I met Bobby Clarke, perennial all-star and three-time most valuable player. Bernie Parent, Hall of Famer, a great goaltender, maybe the greatest of all time. Billy Barber, Reggie Leach, Jimmy Watson, and Moose Dupont were all on the Stanley Cup winning Flyers. I thought, *Wow, I can't believe I'm in this room with all these great players.*

The amazing thing about all that is none of them gave off any superstar vibes or acted arrogant. If you were a fly on the wall in that dressing room, you wouldn't be able to tell who the stars were by how they acted. We were a team, and I was part of that team. It felt amazing to be there like that.

I'm not saying there wasn't a little razzing. The rookie must always endure some of that, but here it was much different than in junior or on the farm team. It was all extremely good-natured.

"Hey, rookie," someone would say, "how about getting me a beer?"

And I'd jump up and go get him a beer. That was about the extent of the hazing, if you could even call it hazing. It felt good. It was fun. No animosity, no threats, no intimidation. It was a refreshing change from what happened in Kalamazoo. Not that it was *all* gentlemanly ribbing. After all, they *did* once wield a pair of scissors menacingly and cut off a chunk of my hair. But, hell, I'll take that over polish on my privates anytime.

As the preseason got underway with exhibition games, I discovered the goalies and the defensemen hung out together on the road. It was almost like they were a mini team within the team. The night before road games, the guys would go to dinner together. Each time they would call to me, "Hey, Behn, you're coming with us." That was sure a nice feeling.

They treated me with respect right from the start, even though I was a brand-new addition to the team. The Flyers had recently won the Stanley Cup, but none of the guys acted superior or gave even a hint that I didn't belong with them.

I roomed with Jimmy Watson that first year. He was a great player, had made the all-star team, and he was always very positive and supportive of me. He looked after me.

If I made a mistake out on the ice, he would try to make me feel better. "Don't worry about it," he would say. "Just move on."

It doesn't sound like much, but his supportive attitude really helped me that first year. Hell, positive support would help in any year.

MY POWER PLAYS WITH CLARKE, BARBER, AND LEACH: A CAREER HIGHLIGHT

OCCASIONALLY OFFICIALS WOULD PENALIZE BOTH TEAMS FOR some infraction or other, and we would have to play a four-on-four game, which is really interesting hockey. With only eight players on the ice instead of ten (I'm not counting goalies here), there is a lot more open ice, which means a lot more room to skate. Defensemen have more of an opportunity to jump into the play offensively and get some scoring chances, maybe even have a three-on-two situation.

Even more exciting is when a penalty is called during a four-on-four. Now it becomes a four-on-three situation. This may be the most exciting scenario in all of hockey. The team with four players can really press their advantage and create great opportunities to score. Four-on-threes are positively electric. You can feel the excitement in the air whenever a four-on-three happens.

From the beginning of my career, I played the power play, five against four. I was usually put out on four-on-three opportunities. I went out with three perennial all-stars: Bobby Clarke, Billy Barber, and Reggie Leach. All three of these guys were amazing all-around players who could handle the puck extremely well.

Barber and Leach also knew if they were carrying the puck, they couldn't get open to shoot because the opposing players would be playing them and cheating on them as much as they could, being a man short. Therefore, Clarke and I carried the puck up the ice most of the time and established control in the opposing end.

Clarke and my job was basically to get Barber and Leach open. They were incredible and renowned as shooters. They didn't really care if an opposing player was putting a stick to my head. If they were open, they wanted the puck on their stick and on time. And for my part, if I got the puck to them where and when they wanted it, I expected to see the puck go into the net. None of us needed "Nice try" or "I almost scored." And our four-on-three power plays generally delivered. Even if one of them took a *hard* shot, it would either score or bounce off the goalie, and then Clarke would get the rebound and put the puck in the net. It was beautiful how it all worked.

When I was on the power play with these three guys, it was like a whole other game. I was a part of a great goal-scoring "team within a team," and I didn't have to worry about the other team's thugs.

One time I was going down the ice, crossing both blue lines, and getting into the other team's zone. Clarke had the puck, but he was getting harassed by a couple of opposing players. I didn't see how he could possibly get the puck to me, so I stopped and began to slip back to defense position.

Big mistake. Somehow, Clarke managed to slide the puck to where I should have been. Only I wasn't there. If I hadn't stopped, the puck would have been on my stick giving me a great goal-scoring opportunity. That was so humiliating that I remember it vividly forty years later. It taught me a lesson: never underestimate these superstars. They can perform miracles. And they did.

Those power plays with Clarke's line were some of the best times I ever had in my entire hockey career.

DEEP THOUGHTS 3

TEAM HIERARCHY

I NEVER HEARD ANY PLAYER IN THE DRESSING ROOM BRAG about the amazing goal they scored, or the sensational save they made. That kind of bragging just never happened. We were all equal.

On the ice, it was a completely different story. There, *everyone* knew exactly who was the best player and where all the other players fit in the hierarchy. I sure did.

The great thing about this hierarchy, from my point of view, is that no one looked down on anyone for not being higher than they were, and no one envied anyone for being higher up. Everyone, and I mean *everyone*, knew we were all doing our absolute best. We were all contributing to the utmost of our ability, and everyone respected that.

We all fought for as much ice time as we could get, but we did it by working on our skills and showing we could compete. I never saw any backstabbing or petty politics among the players trying to play more. All the competition was constructive and healthy. You *wanted* guys on your team who were trying to play more. That was sure better than playing with guys who thought they were down the hierarchy and didn't deserve to play. If you wanted to play, then you showed why you should play. We all did that every chance we got, whether it was in practice or during games.

I fought like hell to get as much ice time as I could, but I knew the guys who were better than me. I was in awe of their talent and skills, their ability to anticipate. I understood they had a gift. I tried to emulate the greats as best I could, but the bottom line was that they were better than me, and hats off to them.

Ice time was a good measure of performance. If you got a lot of ice time, that meant you were valuable to the team, and the coach wanted you out there. In my years with the Flyers, I got a lot of ice time, often almost half the game, so I knew I was one of the better players. Not the top player, but up there.

I also played on power plays and penalty killing. Anyone playing during those key situations was considered a good player. Another crucial time in a game was the last minute or so when we were either down by a goal or up by a goal. You always put your best players on the ice during those situations, and often I was out there.

Later, when I was with Chicago, Doug Wilson got more ice time and crucial ice time than I did on defense. That was fair. He was a better player than me. Like I said, everyone knew where everyone else was on the hierarchy, and I certainly had no resentment toward Doug for his skills and abilities. I was glad he was playing for us and not the other team.

None of it was unfair, and I never saw it that way.

A MILESTONE I DIDN'T WANT TO ACHIEVE

MY FIRST YEAR, I WAS NOT IN ANY FIGHTS IN PRESEASON GAMES. It felt like a miracle. No fighting. Fantastic!

Then the regular season started, and again, in those first few games, I had no fights. No pairing off and punching each other, no dropped gloves, no broken noses, no cuts, no bruises. It was just clean hockey.

Then, just before a game in Boston, Paul Holmgren pulled me aside.

"We had a tough playoff series with Boston last year," he said.

"Okay," I said, not knowing *exactly* where he was going with this, but kind of guessing what was coming next.

"We're going to have to reassert our toughness with this team and not take any of their shit. Can you fight? Because if you can't, then I want you to at least square off with a guy and hold onto him so he can't pair up with one of his guys and go two-on-one on one of our guys."

He wasn't kidding. He really wanted to know if I was up for fighting. If I had it in me. If I had the rage.

I was surprised when he asked me this. Those first few games with the Flyers, I was known as a player, not a fighter. It felt good but strange. I really wanted to be a player and not a fighter. I suppose it was too good to be true.

"I don't know if I can win a fight," I told Paul, "but I will fight."

The game with Boston started out tough but quickly became even tougher when John Wensink ran me into the boards *hard*. Too hard.

I was enjoying my days as a skilled player who didn't fight. It was refreshing and a lot of fun. But I knew there was no way I could survive a long career in the NHL if players could take a huge run at me, like John just did, and get away with it. So he and I got into it.

In my first junior fight, I was sixteen and fighting a nineteen-year-old. Now I was nineteen, stronger, and a much better fighter. Now we were fighting men. The fight with John went well for me. I had my grip and didn't get hit, and I got a few punches on John. In other words, I was a fighter again, and just like that, my days as a non-fighter vaporized forever.

DEEP THOUGHTS 4

WHAT MAKES A GREAT COACH?

MY FIRST OR SECOND YEAR AS A PRO, WE WERE PLAYING AGAINST Montreal. Guy Lafleur was heading down on me on a one-on-one. Guy was the top player in the league back then and I was ready for him. I was not going for any of his fakes, and he was not gonna go around me, period.

He wound up and faked a shot and tried to go past me on the right. I had anticipated he would do this, and I went to the right along with him and tried to cross-check him hard. I had him dead to rights, and I was gonna knock him flying. Everything was set up perfectly in my favor.

Except for one thing.

Somehow Guy leaned backward and slithered past me. Did he pull a *Matrix* on me? It was as slick a move as any spin-o-rama Denis Savard ever pulled. I don't think my glove ever touched Guy, and he scored. Of course.

Defensemen pride themselves on never getting beaten, and I had just gotten beaten in the most dramatic way possible. Every fan and player in the stadium knew it. Especially me.

I went back to the bench feeling absolutely humiliated. How was I going to come back from this? I had let my team down.

Now, most of my previous coaches would've taken this opportunity to employ their keen powers of observation, see what everyone else in the building saw, and yell at me about how bad that play was.

Not my coach Pat Quinn. I was out of breath and sitting on the bench, boiling mad and feeling completely demoralized. Pat walked down the bench and, without saying a word, tapped me on my back, indicating I was to go back on the ice to fill a vacant position.

Let's pause here to take that in.

I had just made an awful play that cost my team a goal. Wasn't I the last person who should be sent out to play the next shift? Not in Pat's opinion. And you know what? He was right. There was no one better to put in the game at that moment.

Why? Because even though I was tired and out of breath from my shift, my adrenaline was pumping hard from my anger, and I was desperate to redeem myself with my team. At that moment, I was the safest guy to put on the ice. I jumped over the boards, took my position, and played hard for the entire shift. Montreal did not score on us.

Pat was my hero for putting me out there. He knew I was feeling horrible about myself, and he gave me a colossal shot of confidence. He gave me the opportunity to keep playing and show what I still had. It was a great thing to do.

That's the art of coaching.

Pat always kept things positive and motivated all of us. It was under Coach Pat that I made the all-star team and that we made it to the Stanley Cup Finals. To me, he was everything a coach should be.

Unfortunately, he was the exception and not the rule. Many of the other coaches I played for were yellers and screamers. They would get in your face and shout at you about any mistakes you made. If you went left on a play, they would yell at you for not going right. If you went right, they would yell at you for not going left. They would yell at you when a puck took a bad bounce on bad ice and skipped over your stick. It was a bad hop, but you still got yelled at. If there was a bad result, you got yelled at, even when you did the right thing. It was exhausting, demoralizing, and paralyzing. It made me hesitate and rethink every single micro decision out on the ice.

Pat saw mistakes. He saw bad hops. But he didn't berate you for them. He figured out how to help a player do better next time.

I get that most coaches were former players, and they probably got yelled at during their playing years, so when they became coaches, that was the only method they knew.

I get it. But it still sucked. I wish more coaches were like Pat.

TIGER WILLIAMS: WELCOME TO THE NHL, BEHN

IN MY FIRST MONTH IN THE LEAGUE, WE WERE PLAYING Toronto when things got a little rough. Guys had thrown off their gloves and were pushing and shoving opponents to try to agitate them. I grabbed onto Tiger Williams, and Tiger wasn't having it. He sucker punched me in the head when I wasn't looking.

I spent the rest of my career aching to get some payback on Tiger for that sucker punch, but as luck would have it, I never got the chance.

Bryan Trottier, a guy I greatly admire as a player and as a human being, has all kinds of great things to say about Tiger. Bryan knew Tiger well, and I certainly respect Bryan's opinions. I just couldn't get over that sucker punch.

Tiger had a long career, twenty years, which is twice as long as mine. He played tough, no question about it, and he caused a lot of shit on the ice. I think he holds the record for most penalty minutes in a career.

To make one thing clear, none of this was personal. I didn't hate Tiger or want him hurt. I had all kinds of respect for him as a fellow tough guy. But the league was the way it was. I couldn't let it be known that I could be run over and I would not do anything about it. As I've said once or twice already, that would have been the end of my career because there would have been no end to the harassment I would have been forced to deal with, and eventually that would have been too much for anyone. Definitely too much for me.

My conclusion about not getting a chance to fight Tiger? He knew how to fight, how to agitate and intimidate. He had agitated me to the point of wanting to take penalties and hurt my team. If he knew that, I'm sure he would be laughing about it maybe to this day.

That's the way life rolls sometimes.

RITUALS

EVERYONE HAD THEIR OWN ROUTINE/RITUAL FOR PREPARING for a game. Most players came to the arena three or four hours before the start of a game. We all checked on our equipment. We made sure our pads and helmets were game ready. We always paid close attention to our sticks.

Every player had their own personal and unique way of taping their sticks. We could hold a stick blindfolded in our hands and tell just by running our fingers over the tape if it was our stick. Most of us had four sticks ready to go for a game. If one broke on the ice, we had spares ready immediately, and during the next break between periods, we would tape up another to replace the broken one. That way we always had four ready to go.

Besides that, everyone had their own way of loosening up and getting ready physically. Some of us stretched, maybe got on the exercise bike. Others walked around the dressing room or the halls, working off some of the nervous energy that can build up before a game.

Some of us were talkers, going nonstop. We told jokes and hurled insults at each other. It was all very good-natured, and most of us ended up laughing at the mild trash talk or lame jokes.

It was nice to have that camaraderie. It lessened the tension, but only a little. By the time we were called out to the ice, we were all pretty wound up. This was serious business. We were paid to win, and we all knew it.

This was all normal, all ritualistic, and all a regular part of the game.

We had similar rituals after the games. Once you've skated hard for the length of a hockey game, there's no way you're going to get to sleep right away. So we'd all go out in whatever city we were in and find a restaurant that stayed open late to have some food. Most of us had not eaten since noon, so we were famished.

If we couldn't find an eatery, which often happened in some Canadian cities, especially on Sundays, we'd look for a bar and go have a few beers. None of us were into any drugs of any kind, but we all liked our beer. We probably drank too much, but it helped us wind down and get ready to sleep.

Even so, I don't think I ever fell asleep before about five in the morning. It took that long to shed all that energy from playing the game. That wind-down felt as much a part of the ritual as anything else we did.

TRAINERS, THE GAME'S UNSUNG HEROES

WHILE WE'RE ON THE SUBJECT OF RITUALS, I WANT TO TALK about trainers, the unsung heroes behind the scenes of every game. General managers deal with players. Coaches deal with the game, and they get a lot of the credit and publicity and sometimes fame.

But without trainers, the games could not happen. Before every single game, our trainer sharpened every player's skates. There are twenty-two guys on a team. That meant sharpening forty-four skate blades. Trainers used a special grinder that made a concave curve in the blade so that each edge of every blade was sharp. No player sharpened their own blades. That was specialized work and required a professional to do it right.

And it had to be right. If your skate was misaligned on the grinder, as sometimes happened, then one edge would be sharper than the other, and that could put you off your best game. On the rare occasions when that happened, we'd take our skate to the trainer between periods or even between shifts, and the trainer would make it right.

Skate sharpening wasn't the only thing trainers did, not by a long shot. When we traveled to games, the trainers packed every player's bags. They knew which player needed a knee brace, which player had to have talcum powder, which one, like me, needed Vaseline to put on his face. They knew all the different needs and wishes of every player, and they packed our bags accordingly.

They also made sure every player got their sticks packed and ready to go. And I'm talking about the game sticks, not the practice sticks, which were usually more worn. They got all this stuff to the airport and on the plane, and when they got to the arena, they got all the bags and all the sticks to the visiting team's locker room, unpacked every bag, and hung up all the stuff in each player's locker.

After a road trip, they gathered up all this equipment and got it back to our home arena, where they hung everything up in our lockers and dried it all out. This often happened at two or three o'clock in the morning, when all of us players were back home in bed.

If we had a morning skate the next day, which we usually did, we arrived about ten or ten thirty, and the trainers were there before eight, sharpening skates and getting equipment ready. It was a tough job, and they don't get enough credit for all they did in support of the players.

This is my shout-out and thank you to them for their hard work and professionalism.

DEEP THOUGHTS 5

FANS

WHAT CAN I SAY ABOUT FANS? PLENTY. FIRST OF ALL, THEY MAKE the league exist. Period. Without them, there would be no NHL.

The vast majority of the hockey fans I knew were great, and I loved playing in front of them. At the same time, there were a few—and I mean *very* few—encounters with fans that were unnecessary.

I remember early in my time with the Flyers, maybe my second game, we were in Detroit. It was the end of the first period, and we were all coming off the ice and walking down the tunnel to our dressing room.

Fans started throwing stuff at us. Empty beer cups, full beer cups. Assorted garbage items. Whatever they felt like they needed to get off their chests, I guess. I raised my hands to protect my head and face from whatever might fall on me. Big mistake because I had my stick in one of my hands. A fan surprised me by grabbing my stick from my hand and hitting me over my head with it.

I suppose you could argue it was my fault for having a stick in my hand. Maybe I should have known there was an asshole fan who would try to hit someone. I guess that's on me. In the moment, I ducked my head and kept going.

I will say that I believe that fan, by bonking me on the head with my own stick, exceeded the rights he obtained when he bought his ticket.

Madison Square Garden fans were famous for throwing coins on the ice. The chances of hitting a player in the eye were slim, but any risk was inexcusable. The real danger is turning hard near the boards, stepping on a coin, and having your skates skip out from under you. Running into the boards like this was very dangerous.

Another time we were hosting Boston in Philadelphia where we had a well-known fan we called the Sign Man. He came with a pile of blank poster boards and some marker pens and made signs on the fly for whatever situation came up during the game.

I got into a fight with Terry O'Reilly, a pretty brutal one that exhausted me. Then, a short time later, Terry and I went at it again. Another brutal fight. Both fights were long and draining.

I was glad to get my five-minute penalty because it meant I could rest up for a while in the penalty box.

I was also hoping I could sit on the bench after my penalty to try to rest up even a little more, but the coach put me out on the ice right away.

We set up for the face-off, and who should be standing right in front of me but Terry O'Reilly. We looked at each other. I was in no condition to fight. I was hoping he was also in no condition to fight.

Then I saw the Sign Man holding up a new sign. It read: *Round Three.*

It's hard to describe how I felt at that moment. It was easy for Sign Man to urge us to get into another fight. He wasn't doing the work. If I'd had the energy, I might have climbed over the glass and pounded on Sign Man for even suggesting Terry and I should pound on each other again.

Terry saw the sign and grinned. Maybe he thought it was funny. Maybe he was thinking about climbing over the glass and going after Sign Man too. I'm not sure. We did *not* fight a third time, for which I am very grateful. And if Sign Man only knew how close he came to getting to meet one or both of us, I'm sure he'd be very grateful too.

It was always great to play home games because the cheering fans always gave the home team an extra boost of confidence and a dependable jolt of energy for the game. It was like having a tailwind at your back. It was wonderful.

Almost all teams play tougher at home, and most guys play better at home. Some scored a lot more at home. I believe that was due to the fans. Just about every team in every sport does better at home, and I have to believe it's because of the fans. They really contribute to the outcome of the game.

The flip side of that, of course, is that you run into a headwind in games at other arenas. All that energy helping the opposing team drags your team down. Most of my fights, by a large majority, were on the road. That was because when you played guys in their own house, they were tougher, filled up with fan energy, and more ready to take you on. That was just a fact.

One thing I never liked was how fans cheered when a player got hurt. That really got to me. The guy sprawled on the ice with maybe a broken limb or something worse was a guy just trying to play a game and provide for his family. There was no call to cheer for that guy getting hurt. Yes, I know I fought to hurt guys, but it was never personal. I would never cheer an injury. Hell, some of the guys on those other teams were my friends, and it hurt when our fans cheered their injury.

Despite that pet peeve, I will say there is nothing more exciting or energy-filling than playing a game with twenty thousand fans cheering you on. It is absolutely one of the most awesome things I experienced in my playing career, and I would not have missed it for anything.

Playoffs were out of this world. When the national anthem ended, the waves of sound coming from the roaring fans were so powerful they could affect your balance.

Another part of the fan experience was fan mail. It was always an honor to get mail from any fan. I remember one letter from a guy who said he had been a hockey fan for thirty years, and he loved seeing me play. It felt good getting that letter. Another fan told me he started getting into hockey because he saw me play, and he got hooked on the game.

Those kinds of interactions were always very positive experiences, and they have not ended. I still get letters from people who somehow dig up my address and send me a hockey card or a picture to sign for them. I always try to answer. It might take a while, and my wife might have to bug me about it, but I try to answer those requests. It is always nice to be remembered after so many decades out of the game.

MY OWN TEAMMATE INJURED ME—WHAT THE FUCK!

DURING PRACTICE A COUPLE OF MONTHS INTO MY FIRST SEASON with Philadelphia, we were all clustered around the coach listening to instructions on what we would be practicing next.

Rick MacLeish thought it would be funny to come up behind me and poke my skates out from under me with his stick. This was completely unexpected, which meant I was unprepared for it. My skates shot out from under me. I fell down on the ice hard and jarred my back and pinched my nerves.

Rick was a fifty-goal scorer and a popular player on the team. He was also on the all-star team for several years. I guess he thought he was a non-fighting goal scorer and that he could do this with impunity. I guess he thought it was funny.

I didn't see it that way. Being a goal scorer and not a fighter, Rick never went after players on the teams we played against. I was supposed to protect him on the ice, but he was allowed to hurt me? An injured back can be devastating to a hockey career. If knocking me to the ice and jarring my back in what amounted to a sucker punch was okay, where would it stop? Maybe poking me in the eye with his stick was going to be the next gut-buster.

It stopped because of what I did next. Our next drill in practice was to work on three-on-ones. That's where three forwards advance on one defenseman. In those situations, the only reasonable play is for the defenseman to stay in the middle to cut down on the angles the shooters have.

I was the defenseman on this particular drill, and Rick was one of the forwards. He had the puck and crossed the blue line with his head down. I saw my opportunity, broke from the center, went after him, and hit him hard. He was caught with his head down and therefore did not protect himself. My hit had to have hurt. Maybe he was as unprepared as I was when he poked my skates out from under me.

Now this was practice, not a real game, but even so, it was about the worst play a defenseman can make in that situation. And you never go after one of your goal scorers.

But I did. The rest of the team was pissed. They must have thought I was either an asshole or crazy. Probably both. I knew I had put myself in a bad position with my teammates. I just didn't care in that situation. My opinion was "Don't fuck with me. Don't fuck with my health. And don't fuck with my career, period. No exceptions."

I did what I had to do. I don't know if I did the right thing. Maybe Rick just lost his sense of humor. What I do know is that he never poked my skates out from under me again.

MY SHOUT-OUTS TO JIMMY WATSON AND TERRY MURRAY

WHEN I WAS IN THE NHL, THERE WAS NO SHORTAGE OF AMAZING skaters, shooters, and stick handlers. A lot of them are famous even today, but there are a lot more really good players who do not get the recognition they deserve.

Part of the reason I wrote this book was to keep the memories of some of those players alive. I'm going to throw in some tribute chapters throughout the rest of the book as my way of giving some of those guys shout-outs to pay them respect for how they played the game.

First up are two of my defense partners, Jimmy Watson and Terry Murray.

I've already mentioned Jimmy. He was my defense partner when I first turned pro. I couldn't have asked for a better partner. He took me under his wing and gave me a lot of confidence, which was a real boost for a rookie coming into the NHL.

Besides all that, Jimmy was a great player. I never saw him play a bad game. He was on the Stanley Cup-winning teams for the Flyers and made the all-star team several times. I would have been honored to play defense with him for my entire career. Unfortunately, Jimmy started having back problems and had to retire way earlier than he should have. He still had a lot of years of good hockey left in him.

Just to give you an idea of what a standup guy Jimmy was to me, I remember one game in my rookie year when we were both out on the ice. I had my head down and Willi Plett, one of the toughest guys in the league back then, elbowed me in the head and just leveled me. Jimmy saw this and came over right away. Jimmy was not a fighter's fighter. He did not stand a chance against Willi, but he didn't care. He saw I got suckered, and he was going to do something about it.

He and Willi got into a fight, and Jimmy got pounded pretty bad. He knew he had no chance against Willi, but he did it for me. That's a standup thing to do as a friend and as a teammate.

Jimmy retired after his eighth season due to his back injury. I only had two years with him as my partner, and it was not enough.

My next partner was Terry Murray, who was older than me by nine years. I was in my third season when he came to the team. Terry had played most of his career in the minors, so he was a seasoned player with lots of experience, and he had a great year.

Terry was an easy guy to play with. He wasn't flashy, but his super-power was that he was steady. He did everything right. He made good passes and was always in position to receive a pass.

We had a good partnership going. I was more offense-minded than Terry, who usually stayed back during a game. This worked well because as he corralled the puck with his stick, he drew opposing players toward him, which left me open to receive his pass. I could then carry the puck into the opposing end or pass it to a forward.

It was a beautiful thing because his passes were *always* accurate and timely, always right on my stick so I didn't have to slow down or reach for them. He was phenomenal that way, and it worked for us all season. For Terry and me, it was definitely a case of one plus one equals three. We were better as a partnership than either of us was on our own.

That was a great year for both of us out on the ice. I was voted to the all-star game that year, for which I give Terry a lot of credit. Just a solid player and a great guy.

With both of these guys, Jimmy and Terry, I look back and think I was the luckiest guy around to have had the privilege of playing with them. We just clicked. It was a great joy to play with them and part of the beauty of playing the game.

COACH BOB "CAGEY" MCCAMMON

LIKE A LOT OF COACHES IN MY HOCKEY CAREER, BOB WAS A screamer. The players all called him "Cagey," I guess because he writhed around like a squirrel in a cage when he got worked up, but I really don't know for sure. He would get in your face and yell at you and tell you what you did wrong while waving his arms in the air. All of this was delivered in a threatening *loud* voice, with him getting red in the face, eyes wide open like a wild man.

It's hard to believe, but being screamed at never helped my game. Not when I was a kid and not in any of the leagues I played in. What it *did* was paralyze me to the point where I just couldn't perform on the ice as well as I knew I could.

Some other players didn't take shit from Bob. He yelled at them, but they yelled right back. "How many Stanley Cups have you won?" they would shout back at him.

Bob was a former player but had never played in the NHL and had never coached a Stanley Cup-winning team, so that was a pretty effective counterattack.

As for me, I was the only rookie on the team. I didn't feel like I had standing to yell back at the coach, so I didn't. I just took his yelling.

A coach should be some combination of mentor, inspiring teacher, and motivator. For Bob, coaching was wrapped up in nonstop yelling.

When I came off the ice at the end of a shift, I could count on Bob screaming at me until my next shift.

It was tough to play well under those circumstances. I felt like, in his eyes, I couldn't do anything right. Whatever move I made, whatever play I tried, he'd find something to criticize about it, and then he would scream it into my ear over and over again.

For me it was awful. And the thing is, we all knew when we fucked up. We were well aware of the missed opportunities, bad moves, and lousy passes. I didn't need him to berate me about it. I was harder on myself than he ever could be.

But when you are constantly criticized in that way, you start to hesitate out on the ice. When you have to make split-second decisions, hesitation will almost always go badly. The yelling, rather than helping me, just kept me from doing my best.

Every game, every period, every shift, Bob was there in my ear as loud and as obnoxious as he could be.

Finally, halfway through the season, during one of these yelling and screaming sessions, where Bob was raining all these insults on me, André "Moose" Dupont turned to him and yelled about as loud as I ever heard Moose say anything, "Leave the fucking kid alone."

Bob wasn't expecting that.

He turned around and walked to the other end of the bench. I love Moose for defending me. It was a pretty nice thing to do for a rookie.

Unfortunately, it didn't last. Next game Bob was back to his old methods. I think yelling was the only thing he knew how to do. I guess he thought yelling was the way to make me a better player, which would help the team. I don't think he ever figured out that all it did was disable me.

I felt like I was fighting the other team and fighting him at the same time.

Funny thing was, while I was getting yelled at, I was also carrying twenty-seven or twenty-eight minutes a game. The most on the team. Why was I carrying so much ice time if my play was so awful?

Coaching is a skill, just like teaching is a skill. I always looked up to my father. He was a great teacher and a great coach. He was able to take a step back from a situation, assess what was going on, and figure out how to nudge a student toward a better result, or nudge me toward a better performance on the ice. That's the kind of coach I wish I'd had for my rookie year. Someone with a special personality, a special way of understanding people and helping them to do better. Yelling did not accomplish any of those things, at least not for me.

To be fair, Bob was not unique in his methods. Many coaches in the league and in other leagues were also yellers, just like that coach who yelled at me when I was just seven years old. It was what they knew. I guess I can't fault them for that, but I do wish they'd had some other methods.

Bob had a long and successful coaching career. He coached the Flyers' farm team and won the Calder Cup championship. He was hired to coach the Flyers when I first turned pro. Pat Quinn was hired as coach of our farm team. Bob got fired three-quarters of the way through my first year, and Pat Quinn took over as our coach. Bob went back to our farm club. A few years later, Pat was fired, and Bob was back coaching the Flyers. Later, after I retired, Pat was the general manager of the Vancouver Canucks and hired Bob to be the coach.

Maybe the yelling really *was* the way to go. Maybe my problems with it were just that: mine.

DEEP THOUGHTS 6

THE TOUGHEST JOB IN SPORTS

DURING GAMES, PLAYERS WERE ALWAYS HOLDING, GRABBING, pushing, and shoving each other. Not to mention the cross-checking and the chipping, high-sticking, and everything else. Hockey was a violent game when I played it, with twelve guys on the ice at any one time, all of them in motion, skating and banging into each other all the time.

The referees have to make instant decisions, sometimes on very subjective grounds, as to what goes too far and what does not. On top of all that, the players and the fans both want absolute consistency *and* a healthy helping of bias, which, let's face it, is impossible. Players naturally pushed and tested the boundaries of what was legal and illegal. Referees were just trying to be consistent. In the playoffs, the refs let a lot more go uncalled. They didn't want to be the ones to determine the outcome of any game.

Sometimes the other team got away with bloody murder on a call, and sometimes our team got called for bullshit. But it also happened the other way around. My take is it all evened out. Referees were never out to get any team or player.

Another thing is that players get breaks between shifts. Officials are out there the entire game. Every second of every minute of every period.

Referees have a tough job, I certainly couldn't do any better, and I'd probably do much worse.

This is not to say I was okay when we got a bad call. It pissed me off, no question. But let's be clear: I was thrilled when the other team got a bad call, so, you know, I hold no grudge against any referee or official who ever worked any of our games. They were all doing their job the best way they could, and I certainly respected them and all their efforts.

LEARNING A NEW POSITION IN FIVE SECONDS

ABOUT HALFWAY THROUGH MY SECOND SEASON AS A FLYER, I was coming off an injury, and I was back for my first game after a few games off. Returning to play under those circumstances is always a nervous time. You're not battle-hardened or game-conditioned anymore. Your timing is usually off, and your stick handling is not as precise. Everything just feels weird, like the game is suddenly some foreign operation, and you're trying to figure it out. My injury was a groin injury, a pulled muscle on my inner thigh. It affected my skating stride, so I wasn't even sure I could skate at 100 percent.

We were playing the Buffalo Sabres, and at one point in the first period, we somehow ended up with only four men on the ice when we should have had five. Something got mixed up on a shift change, and we were missing a right winger. The referee came to our bench and blew the whistle at us. If we didn't get a fifth player on the ice *right now*, he was going to call a penalty for delay of game.

The coach tapped my shoulder. So I jumped the boards, and I was on the ice to play right wing. I had about two seconds, maybe less, to assess the situation and figure out a strategy for a position I had never played in my entire life.

The difference between playing defense and playing forward is like day and night. Forwards were primed for offense. Defensemen were geared for, well, defense. They required very different skills and mindsets. These were not trivial considerations. Hell, I always wanted to be warned if I was going to be playing *left* or *right* defense because even those similar positions required different approaches.

On top of that, I had no game plan. There wasn't any time to put one together. I had to figure out what to do on my own with no advice or coaching.

The other two forwards were superstars Billy Barber and Kenny Linseman. How was I going to keep up with these highly skilled goal scorers? My quick solution: I was going to cause as much disruption on the ice as I could. I was going to be a general pain to the opposing players and try to force a turnover so that Barber or Linseman could then take the puck and score.

The puck dropped, and it was game on. The puck came along the boards, and Larry Playfair of the Sabres blocked the puck to keep it in our end. Not knowing what else to do, I took a run at Larry and tried to cause some shit.

Larry was a big, strong guy. I didn't know if he was a fighter or not. At that time, he might have wanted to drop the gloves and come after me because of the hit I gave him. But that didn't happen. Instead, the puck squirted out and ended up on the other side of the rink on Barber's stick.

I saw my chance. I was faster than Larry, so I began breaking up the ice. I got behind Playfair, and Barber saw it too. He passed me the puck as quickly as he could, figuring I would have a breakaway.

Unfortunately, the pass was just a little bit behind me. I had to slow down a little, drag my foot back, and let the puck hit my skate blade to slide it forward. It worked. I got the puck on my stick. But my slowing down for that instant gave Larry a chance to catch up to me. He tackled me, and I went down. Larry got called for a penalty, and I was awarded a penalty shot.

Penalty shots are pretty rare. Hockey can go a whole season, or even seasons, without even one penalty shot. They are only awarded when a player is on a clear breakaway, like I was, and the opposing player cuts him down from behind, like Larry did in this case. Penalty shots for a defenseman are even more rare. Practically unheard of.

But I got one. Like I said, I was feeling a little rusty after my injury, so I went to the bench before taking the shot and squirted some water on my face to buy time.

Players hardly ever discussed penalty shots. I guess because they were so rare, no one much felt like we needed to have a strategy for them. Some of us worked on them for fun after practice sessions, but that was about it. I never expected to get a penalty shot. Except on that night, I did.

Guys with big slap shots, if they ever got a penalty shot, would just let loose with a hard shot from point-blank range. It was different for me. Sure, I scored some goals, but I didn't have a great slap shot, something I learned when I tried to keep up with Doug Wilson. I figured I would rely on my instincts. No plan. Should I just shoot from point blank as well? Maybe try to deke and hope to get the goalie moving the wrong way?

I skated to center ice. The puck was there waiting for me. The linesman blew the whistle, and I was off. I skated fast toward Bob Sauvé, an excellent goalie. He was a good distance forward of the net, trying to cut down my angles. Since I was a defenseman, would he be guessing I would be more comfortable just taking a slap shot? Did he think I was going to rely on a deke? Was I going to do a double reverse? What was Bob's strategy?

With no plan in my head, as I got closer to the net, I thought I saw a corner I could hit. As I wound up to take my shot, I noticed that Bob was staying far out from the net and not backing in.

Half surprising myself, I stopped completing the shot. I had Bob frozen a little too far out of the net. I did a couple of shifts, shuffling the puck on my stick, and went around to the side. Bob could not back up in time. I had an open net.

I took the shot.

Because I was not playing at 100 percent, I only got the puck about a foot off the ice when I should have been able to hit the top corner. It didn't matter. All Bob could do was put out his stick and hope to stop the puck. He came close. The puck hit his stick, but not enough to stop it from going in. It bounced off his stick and ended up in the net.

I was as surprised as anyone that my fake shot worked and I got a goal. I had been playing organized hockey since I was five years old, and I had never had a penalty shot before or after. I ended my career one for one on penalty shots. You can't get much better than 100 percent. Maybe I should have been a penalty shot coach. One thing is for sure: my brief career as a right winger turned out to be memorable.

OUR HISTORIC UNBEATEN STREAK

HOCKEY HAS SUPERSTARS, OF COURSE. WE ALL KNOW THEIR names: Gretzky, Messier, Trottier, Dryden, Lemieux, and so on. But all those great players are part of teams, and sometimes teams can become as famous and dominating as any player.

Case in point: the Philadelphia Flyers in the 1979–1980 season, my second year on the team. We went thirty-five straight games without a loss, which I believe is still an all-time NHL record and a professional sports record.

Of course, as you're putting together a streak like that, every other team knows it, and they come gunning for you. Every team wants to be the team that stops the streak.

We didn't make it easy for them. We just kept winning. And funny thing, it's easier to be winning than losing. When you're ahead in the game, you can just dump the puck into the opposing end and let the game play on. When you're down a goal or two, the last few minutes of the game can be exhausting. The coach plays the top players a lot, trying to get some offense going. It turns into a grind where the top players finish the game exhausted.

When you're leading the games, that doesn't happen. You finish the game without burning all your energy reserves. And when this happens game after game, it makes hockey a hell of a lot of fun.

As it happened, I missed the first dozen or so games of this streak due to an injury. And even a dozen unbeaten games in a row is something to take note of. When I recovered enough from my injury to play, I knew one thing: it wouldn't make me look good if we lost the streak on my first game back.

I was rusty and I knew it, but nevertheless I overextended myself and got caught up the ice, out of position. The other team put together a quick odd-man rush and took the puck up the ice on our goalie.

This was my fault. No question.

Not knowing what else to do, I whacked the guy on their team who was standing near me. We got into a fight, and the ref immediately blew the whistle. Their odd-man rush was stopped on the spot.

My asshole move stopped their goal. We went on to win the game and keep the streak going, so all was well. No one seemed to remember that I got us into a bad situation by being out of position.

The streak went on. And went on and went on. We were riding high, and we all loved every minute of it. There is no better feeling than winning, and no worse feeling than losing. When you lose a game and you don't play for another two or three days, it affects every part of your life. You don't feel like doing anything for fun. It's just this misery that sets in, and you can't shake it.

We never had any of *that* during our unbeaten streak. It was all amazing, invigorating, and just plain fun. Too bad every season couldn't be that way.

DEEP THOUGHTS 7

RAGE: DON'T LEAVE HOME WITHOUT IT

I'VE ALREADY TALKED ABOUT RAGE IN THIS BOOK, BUT IT IS worth visiting again because it is such an important part of being a fighter. Rage is the ability to instantly draw on your adrenaline for maximum strength. You need that strength and energy for at least thirty seconds and sometimes up to two minutes.

During that rage time, you use all your energy and conserve nothing. All the best fighters had it. I know I had it throughout my career. I could summon rage whenever I needed it. It was a natural part of my being.

When the rage came on me in a fight, it was like being in an altered state. I almost felt like I was someone else, someone seized by this *thing*. Guys who saw me fight had a saying. They said, "Behn snapped." That's as good a description as any. The rage snapped me into another state of being.

Lots of fighters, when they first came up to the NHL, had the rage, but for most players it was short-lived. Few of them had reliable rage for more than a couple of seasons. Two of the best ones, the guys who could bring the rage year after year after year over a long career, were Terry O'Reilly and Willi Plett. I give those two guys all kinds of respect because they fought their entire careers, and they always had maximum rage.

Where did they get their rage? Where did I get mine? My best guess is that it was just innate. An ability we were born with.

There is no training for rage in hockey. No training for fighting. Before junior hockey I never got into a fight. They didn't allow it in the lower leagues. When I got to junior, lots of guys fought. I got into many, many fights. For a lot of guys who had relatively marginal skills, fighting was a good way to make themselves more valuable to a team. Having fighting on your résumé was a value-add. Lots of guys figured that out and learned to fight.

I count myself lucky for learning to fight in junior. Here's why. Many players in junior didn't fight. They didn't have to. They had good skills and contributed without fighting, so they were never forced to learn. Then, when they made the NHL, they were not top players anymore, since the league had all kinds of *great* players, the very best in the world. Once that realization set in, some of these guys figured out that to give added value to the team, they should learn to fight.

Bad timing. Learning to fight while in the NHL should be avoided at all costs! Guys who tried usually got pounded a few times and then gave up. It was too much. Experienced fighters had too much of everything: strength, size, rage, intimidating presence, and, most of all, experience. They'd been fighting in the league for a while. For the new guys, trying to learn fighting against these guys just got them a lot of hard blows to the head.

For me and other guys who fought in junior, we already knew how to fight. We came to the NHL with strategy and tactics under our belts. I had already learned to hold onto the other guy's elbow. I already knew to bring up the rage and pepper the guy with quick hits right at the start of the fight to disorient him. By the time I hit the NHL, I had all that figured out. I came equipped.

And it wasn't just that I had the skills. The whole idea of fighting was hardwired into me by that time. I knew not to let anyone push my goaltender around. I knew not to let anyone roll over my defense partner. All of that was so ingrained in me that even though I was a good player without the fighting, by that time I was a fighter. I was the one they called on to answer the bell when their top fighter pounded on one of our guys.

Let me digress here a little and say that this was nothing I ever wanted. I didn't *want* to be a fighter. I would much rather have been in hockey as a good player who never had to fight. It would have been easier on my body and my mind. Fighting was a game that drained me. It took all my energy, and then, after the fight, I had to rally and play the real game, the hockey game. I was able to do both year after year, but many players couldn't.

Here's another aspect to all this. Non-fighters were always in greater danger than fighters of getting hit with a cheap shot. Opposing players went after non-fighters since they knew they could get away with it.

Kenny Linseman once got cross-checked so bad he lost teeth and broke his jaw and had to get it wired. He was not a big guy, and he was not a fighter, and the guy who crossed him knew that. Kenny paid the price. He received a career-threatening injury, while the cross-checker got a two-minute penalty, maybe five minutes. That was how the fight game was played. It was unfair, but that was what it was. If you didn't fight, you carried significant risks.

Some guys excelled at fighting. They honed their fighting skills just like superstars honed their shooting skills. The players with fewer skills but who fought a lot were called *goons* if they were on the other team. This was a derogatory term. Players like that on your own team, well, that was different. Our fighters who were maybe of the same caliber we called *tough guys*. I think if you squint and tilt your head sideways, you can see the subtle but very real difference between a goon and a tough guy.

Back then, with the game so violent and penalties not being called as they should, fighting was a big part of a team's success. Guys like me, who were willing to punch it out at the drop of a glove and were good at it, were definitely sought after. Fighting was an asset to the team, but it was also personal. I was always willing to go first into the corner to play the puck. Going first left you vulnerable to being run over from behind.

Sometimes I had my head down in those situations, so you could argue any consequences were on me because I did not stay hyper-alert. But. You'd better hope that I didn't get up off the ice, because if I did, I was going to hurt you worse than you were going to hurt me.

And I did exactly that. I learned early on that was how the fighting game was played. I went with it, and it worked for me. Rage was my friend.

Not that it was healthy for me. It wasn't. There were very real downsides.

Case in point: gloves. They are cesspools of bacteria. It comes from all the sweat that you produce as you're playing the game. All kinds of dirt, dried blood, and assorted shit gets into your glove, and there isn't much you can do about it. I would stick my hands into my gloves and practically feel the little bacteria buggers ready to pounce on any cut I might have and give me a nasty infection.

And boy did I have cuts. When you were into a fight, bare-knuckled as we were, you inevitably got cuts on your fingers and the back of your hands.

After the game, I taped up my cuts and treated them to try to help them heal. I left the tape on during practice, but when the next game came along, I had to take off the tape because if I had tape on my hands during a fight, I would get suspended. Taped hands were not allowed.

This meant I put my hands, which were just starting to heal, back into the bacterial soup of my gloves, and as the game went on, the scabs scraped off, leaving me bleeding again, and the infections rees-tablished themselves.

It also hurt like hell to play with cut hands, sometimes so bad that I could barely wrap my glove around the end of my stick. But I did it. I pushed that pain away and got on with the game. Cuts on knuckles that would normally heal in a couple of weeks could last months and months during a hockey season. All cuts got infected.

Yes, the glamour of playing rough hockey was a never-ending blessing and joy.

MY SHOUT-OUT TO WILLI PLETT, WHO SHORTENED MY CAREER

I PLAYED AGAINST A LOT OF TOUGH GUYS IN MY CAREER. THE league was crawling with them when I was in it. But without question, the absolute toughest guy I encountered was Willi Plett.

I first ran into him in my rookie year when he played right wing for the Atlanta Flames. I studied his stat sheet before the game and saw he already had some good years, even scoring forty goals the previous season. He was also blond, like a Swede.

Swedes weren't known as fighters. This was mostly because they came from playing in Europe, where the rinks were bigger, penalties were called, and there was just a lot more room to play hockey rather than get into fights.

Taking all that into consideration, and looking at his kind of foreign-sounding name, I figured Willi for a Swedish goal scorer.

That was my first mistake.

Near the start of the game, Willi came skating around the back of our net, preparing to loop around in front. I was there, and I speared him real hard, thinking, *This Swedish goal scorer won't ever be scoring on me.*

That was my second mistake.

A split second later, Willi dropped his gloves, and I found out the hard way he was not a goal-scoring Swede but rather a tough fucking fighter, clearly seasoned by many previous fights. He had the rage. In spades. And I quickly realized I was fighting for my life.

Over the course of our careers, he paid me back for that spear. We ended up having eight fights, all of them exhausting epics, full of hard punches with no holds barred. He cross-checked me more than once to the back of my neck and even got a stick in my face once that required stitches to sew up.

When I look over the history of our fights, they went pretty well. And by pretty well, I mean I usually had a good to great grip on his punching arm and was able to keep him from putting his fist through my skull. One slip-up, one mistake, and that was exactly what would have happened. Willi was in it to win.

The fact that I more or less won the first few fights should have made Willi back down. That sure as shit did not happen. It did exactly the opposite. He was so pissed off that he hadn't put me down that his rage elevated to what I'll call double rage. During our fourth or fifth fight, fists flying, some landing, some not, Willi stopped throwing punches and decided he was going to rip my helmet off, all the better to batter my skull.

He grabbed me and started shaking me. I lost my balance, which made me lose my signature grip on his elbow. That gave him a free hand to punch me hard in the back of my head. It opened up a cut that later required a few stitches. The guy really rang my gong. He knocked me dizzy.

The smart thing to do in that situation is to stay down. Let the referees jump in. No point in getting up and trying to fight when you're dizzy. That's just nuts. You're an easy target as you're rising up in that condition.

So what did I do? Of course I got up. I was dizzy, sure, but I had the rage. Big time. I reestablished my grip on Willi's elbow, and I started punching. I caught him with one or two good punches, and I cut him for stitches. Instant payback for the cut he just gave me.

I was still dizzy, but I felt his strength dissipate. We were both hurt, but I wasn't giving up. I kept yanking on his jersey, yelling at him, and trying not to show I was hurt. I kept yelling and didn't stop until Billy Barber, my teammate, came over to me.

"Hey, Behn," he said. "Willi's already off the ice."

I blinked. I was so dizzy from the hit Willi had given me that I didn't know what I was doing. I had no idea whose sweater I had in my grip. No idea Willi was no longer on the ice.

The linesman escorted me to the exit. I was still so dizzy and disoriented, I don't think I could have found the exit on my own. The world was spinning. I didn't even know where I was putting my skates down. On the rubber mat they laid out over the concrete? On the concrete? I didn't know. It was incredibly disorienting.

My cut was hidden by my hair. Willi's cut was right on his face. He looked like he was injured. I looked fine.

That's a tough way to win a fight, and it wasn't our last one. Willi and I went at it hard several more times. No one in my career was a tougher fighter than Willi. He gets all kinds of respect from me. Over the years, I threw everything I had at Willie. He didn't back down one inch.

INCHES FROM THE HOLY GRAIL BUT STILL GUTTED

NO ONE SAID HOCKEY WAS GOING TO BE EASY, AND I NEVER expected it to be. My first year I kept my head down, worked hard, and did what I could to contribute. We had a pretty good season, and then it was the next season. My second year as a Flyer.

We had a great year with that record-breaking unbeaten streak, made the playoffs with ease, and got through the early rounds. Then we were in the finals against The New York Islanders.

We had Clarke, Barber, and Leach as our main line. New York had a great line, too, putting Bryan Trottier, Mike Bossy, and Clark Gillies up against us. Backing up our top line, we had all kinds of great players like Kenny Linseman, Brian Propp, Paul Holmgren, Mel Bridgman, Jimmy Watson, and Moose Dupont. We had a very hot Pete Peeters in goal.

Not to be outdone by those guys, the Islanders boasted solid players behind their line, guys like Butch Goring, John Tonelli, Bob Nystrom, and most of all, Denis Potvin, one of my early hockey heroes who you will remember as my favorite player back in the first chapter of this book. They also sported all-star Billy Smith in goal.

I list all these players just to let you know the caliber of talent in that series. It was set up to be an exciting series, and I expected to see and be in some great hockey.

Some of our guys who had been on Stanley Cup-winning teams previously told me I needed to get ready. The final series was not like any other series. Those games were not like any other games. To play well, you really had to up your skills. You had to prepare. "You never know if you will get another shot at the Stanley Cup," said my teammates. I got it. I was ready.

Bryan Trottier, who has been on a lot of Stanley Cup-winning teams, said in his book *All Roads Home* that the finals are a whole new thing, a whole new game. I agree with Bryan wholeheartedly. It isn't just the extra stress and intensity knowing you're playing for the ultimate hockey trophy. To me, the whole experience was otherworldly. Fighting was kept to a minimum or was nonexistent. No one wanted to get a penalty for fighting that might lead to a game-winning goal in the finals. We were out there playing hockey, and it was glorious.

The series lived up to its potential. Both teams played good hockey, and we got to the sixth game. We were down three games to two and now playing in New York. This meant we had to win this game to take the series back to Philadelphia, where we would then have a good chance at the Cup. For New York, they just had to win this, their home game.

Going into the third period, we were tied. We actually should have been ahead because one of the Islander goals came on an offside play that wasn't called by the officials. But bad calls are part of the game, and you can't let it get to you. The Islanders didn't cheat or anything. If we had been the beneficiaries of a bad call, we would have taken it. Any team would.

Anyway, still tied at the end of the third period, we were going into overtime. Sudden death. The first team to score a goal would win the game. For the Islanders it would be a Stanley Cup–winning goal. For us it would be a chance to play one more game that season.

Everything is ramped up in overtime. The tension, the intensity reaches high levels of stress. Every pass is crucial. Every move you make could be the end.

As luck would have it, New York scored in the overtime period.

It's hard to explain how our loss devastated me. I was on the bench, gasping for air, trying to get ready for my next shift. They had the puck and were rushing toward our end. Then, the arena erupted in a deafening explosion of noise. I knew what that screaming meant.

I just remained on the bench for some time. I don't know how long. I was no longer tired, no longer amped up for my shift, no longer ready to contribute. It felt like I was having an out-of-body experience, a hollowed feeling of numbness.

I give the Islanders all kinds of credit for their win, which, as it turned out, was the first of four in a row for them. Like I said, they were a great team.

No one likes to lose, and no one likes to lose the Stanley Cup finals. Nothing to do about it. No pill to take. No words to help. All you can do is just try to get over it during the summer and come back the next season ready to go again.

VOTED TO THE ALL-STAR GAME

I WAS IN MY THIRD SEASON WITH THE FLYERS, AND I WAS HAVING a good year. I was voted to the All-Star Game in the middle of the season.

All-Star Games are not brutal affairs. There isn't fighting or egregious cheap shots or any of that kind of thing. It's a bunch of guys who love hockey just going out to play a highly skilled game. It doesn't mean anything in the standings.

When I was voted on the team, a reporter asked me how I felt. "I'm very proud," I said.

Then they asked Billy Barber, who also made the all stars, how he felt. His answer was way better than mine. He said, "I'm very honored."

As soon as I heard that, I thought, *That's what I wanted to say.* And it was what I *should* have said.

To this day it bothers me that I didn't give a similar answer to Billy's. Maybe someone could have coached me on what to say. Actually, there's no maybe about it. We *should* have gotten instruction on dealing with the media, the reporters, and the sportswriters. But it was just like everything else in the league: on-the-job training. You figured it out on your own, or you didn't.

Some guys like Billy were naturals at speaking with the press. They knew how to stay positive and give good answers. Jimmy Watson was like that too. He was a natural. I, on the other hand, was not a natural, though I learned as I went along in my career. I learned not to put my foot in my mouth or say stupid things when reporters came to me after games and threw questions at me.

Aside from the fact that getting voted to the all-star team *is* a real honor because it means the voters consider you one of the best players in the league, there was one other aspect of the game that meant a lot to me.

From the time I was in junior hockey all the way to the end of my career, I always put Vaseline on my face before a game. Between periods, I freshened up that Vaseline and made sure it was on good and thick. Why would I do this? So if I got into a fight and someone hit me with their fist or gloved hand or whatever, there was more chance the hit would slide off me instead of opening up a cut on my face.

I knew I wouldn't be getting into any fights in the All-Star Game. No one was going to whack me over the head and then get into a fair fight with me while I was down on the ice. That wasn't going to happen. It felt both weird and good to not have to protect myself in that way. The one and only game I didn't feel the need to protect myself with a coat of Vaseline was that one All-Star Game.

Okay, but even though I knew I didn't *have* to, I still did it. I couldn't help it and still put the Vaseline on my face.

The game itself was glorious. We did not practice as a team before the game, but that didn't matter. We were all experienced and skilled players. We knew the language of hockey, and we spoke it fluently that night.

It was what hockey should be. We all skated hard and fast, and we moved the puck with quick, snapping passes that hit their targets with precision. It was just a crisper and more awesome game than what happened during the regular season. The ice was crawling with superstars, so why wouldn't it be a great game?

At one point, Gretzky and I were on the ice rushing up the rink. I had the puck, and we did a give and go, and I ended up with the puck very near their net all alone. My instincts just kicked in, and faster than you can blink, I did a couple of quick dekes, and the puck ended up past the goalie and in the net. I just stood there thinking, *Holy shit, did that just happen? Did I just score a goal in the NHL All-Star Game?*

As much as it was a personal career highlight for me, I am sure it was just another All-Star Game for Gretzky, and I am sure he has no recollection of his great pass at all.

DEEP THOUGHTS 8

NO ONE LIKES TO BE OWNED

FROM THE TIME I WAS SEVEN YEARS OLD, SOME TEAM OWNED the rights to me. In kid leagues, the coaches said where and when I played. When the 67s drafted me, I had two choices: play for them or quit hockey. There was no other option. When the Flyers drafted me, it was the same thing: play for them or quit hockey. And when I got traded to Chicago, with no input from me: play for them or—well, you know.

At the time, I just figured that was the way it was. When I was a kid, no one ever asked me if I was ready to move away from my family and play in another city. "Would you rather play for the Toronto Marlboros and live at home?" That question never came up.

No one ever asked me if I was ready to move to Philadelphia, a city in a country different from where I grew up. Later, no one ever asked me if I was okay with uprooting my family and moving to Chicago, where we had no connection with the community. No one ever asked me any of those things, and I knew not to say anything because whatever team I was on *owned the rights to me*. Period.

Maybe I should have had the choice to offer my services to another team if I wanted to. After all, if I was a salesman at one car dealership, there would be nothing stopping me from quitting and going to work for another dealership on the other side of town if that was what I wanted to do and if they were willing to hire me. Hockey players did not have that luxury. If I said no to one team, I would have said no to every team. No other organization could hire me, and my hockey career would have been done.

For a sports professional, this state of affairs was just part of the game. I didn't like it, but there it was. You moved on to the next team and did your best there.

The players, of course, were completely different from management. When I came to a new team, all the guys were welcoming and fabulous. Guys you used to fight with became your teammates and buddies. It was wonderful. I only have good things to say about any of them.

BACK-TO-BACK FIGHTS IN CHICAGO

I WAS UNDER NO ILLUSIONS THAT WHAT HAPPENED IN THE ALL-Star Fame, where everyone was playing good, clean hockey instead of chipping and tripping and fighting and brawling, was going to carry over into the regular season. I returned to play defense for the Flyers and got into some fights relatively quickly.

By that time in my career I was more or less resigned to fighting being a part of my game. I was pegged as an enforcer, a fighter, and I had to deal with that reputation. Believe me, sometimes I wished it was otherwise, but we don't always get to choose what happens in our lives, and I couldn't stand anyone on my team getting pushed around.

I remember one night in Chicago. I got into a fight. I don't even remember who I was fighting anymore, and it doesn't really matter. It was a typical fight: gloves off, fists flying. By the time it ended, I was exhausted as usual and was escorted to the penalty box by the linesman. I figured with the fight over, I was going to get to rest up a little before my next shift on the ice. But Chicago, for some reason, didn't want to let it go.

Their players were yelling at me. Why? I don't know. Maybe they were acting tough. Maybe they didn't like the outcome of the fight. Who knows? The officials held the Chicago players back, but next thing I knew, a Blackhawks player slipped by a linesman and came after me, ready for another fight. My second fight in just a couple of minutes.

I was exhausted. This guy was fresh off the bench. That was not any kind of fair fight, but what could I do? I had to fight back. I had to summon the rage all over again and go at it with this guy.

I had a few thoughts going through my head. How did the officials let this happen? Where was my team? I was out there on my own. Did they think this was easy for me? Did they think I was having a good time having back-to-back fights?

I didn't have any answers then, and I don't have any answers now. What I did have was one thought: *What am I doing here? This is crazy. How did I get here? How is this fighting normal?*

It made no sense.

Earlier, in another fight, I was about to hit a guy pretty good. I was winning the fight, and I was sure I was going to put him down hard. What happened? A linesman grabbed me and held my punching arm. But that left my opponent completely unrestrained. Pretty much a two-against-one fight, which gave the other guy an opportunity to hit me.

How was that fair? The linesman was trying to level the playing field, so because I was winning, he figured the thing to do was let the other guy get in some free punches? Do you hold back Muhammad Ali because he's about to knock out George Foreman?

Maybe they should have called a penalty whenever a goal scorer lifted his stick to take a shot. After all, that would have evened things up. The goal scorer should not get the advantage of getting to score a goal. Have to make things fair, right? Obviously *not*.

So how was it fair to let this second Blackhawks player come after me?

The officials have a tough time making calls. I get that. But when I was in that second fight, so tired I could barely stand, running on pure rage energy, it just felt completely wrong. All of it.

I truly wondered, *What am I doing here?*

DEEP THOUGHTS 9

ICE, ICE, BABY

IT'S NOT A DEEP THOUGHT TO KNOW THAT HOCKEY NEEDS ICE. There's a lot more to it, though. Remember the story of my dad and the neighborhood rink he built every winter? He knew that you build up ice thin layer by thin layer. You don't just flood an area with a lot of water and expect to have good ice you can skate on and play hockey on.

It's the same thing in organized hockey. Good ice takes time to make. It must be made layer by layer. When I was in the NHL, many of the arenas I played in were dual purpose. They hosted both basketball and hockey games. One of two things would happen. They would cover up the ice with boards to make a court for basketball. Or they would take out the ice for basketball.

In the former case, basketball players hated it because the floor was very cold from the ice under it, and that cold would go up their legs and make their knees ache.

If they took out the ice for basketball instead, we hockey players hated it because it often meant not enough time between events to properly make ice. It happened far too often.

When you flood an area in one shot, you don't get good skating ice. Instead of a hard surface, you get crystallized water instead, and it is weak. It can't withstand the force of the hockey players skating on it.

Often, playing on ice like that, when we had to put on the brakes, our skate blades cut into the ice, and we went right through it to the concrete below. That in itself is dangerous enough because believe it or not, concrete will rip the skates out from under you. Without the ice to hold your skate edge, your feet just shoot out from underneath you. If your momentum is taking you to the goalposts or boards, you have a strong chance of being hurt.

But there's more. Imagine twelve big, hard-skating hockey players shredding the low-quality ice surface by braking hard, digging in, and turning hard. Before long the ice is grooved and chipped, no longer a smooth surface. It was precarious to play a game on that kind of surface.

I remember a few times I had the puck and had to go behind my own net to keep it away from the opposing team. The ice gets especially chewed up in that narrow area, and the puck bounced like crazy on the rough ice. I had to be careful not to get tripped up on grooves and gullies there. Sometimes just keeping upright on my skates was a little precarious, and holding onto the puck was just a crapshoot. Someone would pass you the puck and you'd be all ready to receive it, and then it would hit a groove in the ice and bounce over your stick. Suddenly the other team had a breakaway because you couldn't keep the puck. All due to ice conditions.

We had to play on this kind of ice all the time in our own arena and in places like Madison Square Garden. Both teams had to deal with it because there was nothing we could do, but we hated it. When you have lousy ice, a lot of snow accumulates, especially around the boards. This changes the game. Instead of the puck bouncing off the boards in a normal way, the puck encounters the berm of snow and bounces *up* the board instead.

This means toward the end of the period, before the Zamboni came out and groomed the ice and got rid of the snow, the play was very different. We had to keep our heads down more to know where the puck was going. This meant we weren't as aware of where the other players were on the ice.

Nowadays, the Zamboni will sometimes come out during the period, which must help considerably.

One arena that never had any of these problems was in Minneapolis. I guess they didn't have a basketball team sharing the arena, which meant their ice was always hard and smooth and flat, a pleasure to play on.

Behn and older brother in backyard skating rink

Me with Kristie and Bernie

Behn waterskiing

Keith Brown

Behn with Ellie, Kristie, and Vicki

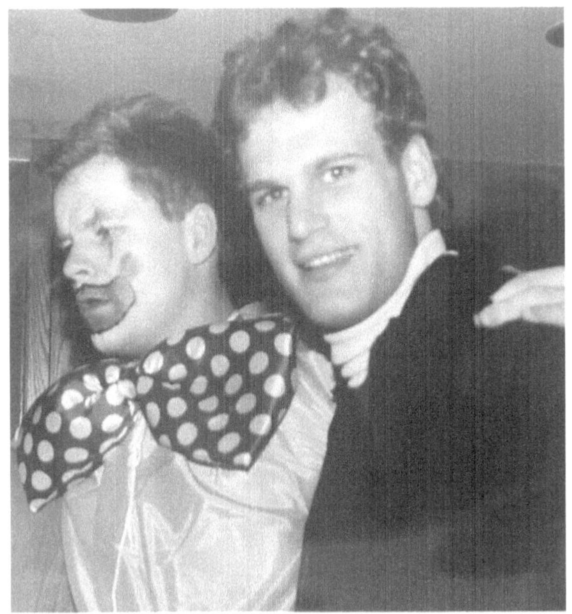

Gary Nylund

My pride and joy, Kristie, Ellie, and Victoria

Behn and Rita

Behn with Bernie Parent

My dad and me with my kids on the "Pirate Ship"

Curt Fraser

Just another superfan of mine. I think his name is Mario

Austin, Behn, and Christian

Rita, Behn, Gini, and Bernie

Rita and me with two grinches, Christian and Austin

Kristie, Behn, and Brent with two superstars, Christian and Austin

Behn (2Bob) with grandchildren Hudson and Owen

Behn and Rita

Kristie, Brent, Behn, and Rita

Doug Wilson and daughter Lacey

Ellie, Kristie, and Victoria

Rita and Behn

Behn and Bernie, mano a mano

Behn and daughter, Ellie

MY SHOUT-OUT TO TIM KERR AND THE DAY I WRESTLED WITH SUPERMAN

I KNEW TIM WHEN WE PLAYED TOGETHER IN JUNIOR. HE WAS two years younger than me when he made the team at only fifteen years old. Tim was a big guy. My brother and I were big guys, both six feet three inches tall, and we weighed in at about 210 pounds then. Tim was the same height, but he weighed a good 215 pounds and had absolutely no fat. Just muscle. Later he got a little bigger, maybe 230 pounds, but again, he was ripped. Not an ounce of fat on him.

He played center in junior, and that was what he played when he came to the Flyers. No one could move Tim. He was a whole level of power above the rest of the league. If he was in front of the net, he stayed in front of the net. He didn't get pushed aside by anyone. All you had to do was get the puck to him, and he could score. He had many fifty-goal seasons.

One of my stories about Tim makes me look bad, but I'll tell it anyway. We were playing in Montreal, and for some reason I can't figure even today, I told Tim that Bill Baker, a Canadiens defenseman, was pushing Tim around.

"Tim," I said, "this is getting embarrassing. He's making you look weak. You can't let this go on. You can't let him humiliate you like that." And so on. I laid it on pretty thick, and I was kind of relentless.

None of this made any sense at all because it had nothing to do with reality. Bill Baker was *not* pushing Tim around. That was just something I made up. I sure didn't expect a fight to come out of my bullshit, but I must have been pretty convincing because Tim got all fired up and fought with Baker.

Tim was not a fighter. This was the only fight I ever saw Tim get into, and Tim had strength you didn't see in the NHL back then. I won't say he almost killed Bill, but he did beat him pretty bad. After the fight, I think Baker must have wondered what the hell just happened. I don't blame him. He didn't deserve the beating he got.

I thought I was just having fun with Tim, but the upshot is it could have ruined Bill Baker's career. That was absolutely not my intention, but it taught me a lesson: don't unleash Tim Kerr on anyone. Or maybe I should?

On the plus side, since this was Tim's first year in the NHL, I helped him quite a bit by making him look tough. I'm not going to say it was because of the fight I inadvertently started, but no one messed with Tim after that. Draw your own conclusions.

My other story about Tim took place a little later, after I was traded to Chicago and Tim was still playing for Philadelphia, but I can't resist telling it here.

I was a Blackhawk playing in my old arena in Philadelphia. Tim and I were tied up in the corner at our end.

One of the points of pride I picked up for myself as my career went along was that I always had physical control of my own corner. I worked to never let anyone outmuscle me in my territory. It was *my* territory, and I was going to dominate. I was always going to tie up the opposing player so they didn't have a chance in hell of scoring on us.

Well, this particular night, on this particular occasion, it was Tim's turn. For some reason, he decided he was going to tie *me* up. In *my* corner.

This made absolutely no sense. He was a forward. His job was to score goals, not tie up a defenseman in his own end.

I'm not exaggerating when I say this was an unnerving experience.

Everything was wrong. Tim held me against the boards, and I couldn't move. I couldn't get away from him, and I couldn't escape his grip. He had me pinned. I was embarrassed that there was nothing I could do. He was too strong for me.

I've had a few out-of-body experiences in my life. This was one of them. I felt like I didn't have control of my own body.

So I stopped trying to wrestle him. I was still trapped. Still looking to get out of the situation. I didn't even know where the puck was by then. If I had held Tim that long, I would have gotten called on a holding penalty. Only the officials didn't call a penalty. It was just Tim keeping me in place, not letting me do anything.

And that was when he just started laughing.

Now, laughing in the middle of a game was absolutely crazy. What the hell was Tim laughing about? What was going on?

Tim released me and stepped back.

"Hey, buddy," he said. "I am Superman." And then he skated away, still laughing.

That was a humbling experience. A real shock to my system. Being dominated like that in my own end was almost more than I could stand.

But it happened. It showed me Tim was a powerful athlete. Something I already knew, but not in the way I knew it at that moment. The guy was a physical monster.

I was lucky Tim wasn't a fighter. My dominating tactic of grabbing the inside of a guy's elbow wouldn't have worked with Tim. He was a lefty. Holding down his right arm wouldn't have helped me, and holding down his left arm wouldn't have left my punching arm free. Of all the guys in the league, fighters and non-fighters, Tim was the one I would least want to fight. Ever. He was powerfully built, and he was a lefty. A deadly combination.

None of what happened between us in the corner that game changed our friendship one bit. We were friends before and remained friends after. We still stay in touch to this day.

DEEP THOUGHTS 10

ZEN AND THE ART OF CROSS-CHECKING

HITTING AND BODY CHECKING IN HOCKEY IS NOT SOME RANDOM violent act. It is very purposeful. You run hard at players to intimidate and disrupt their game. If you could intimidate them with aggressive play, then they might be reluctant to go full force into the corner after a puck. They might instead go in soft, a little less likely to mix it up with me or someone else. When that happened, when a guy could be scared into being more wary or more unwilling to get hit, it meant I did my job.

Now, of course, it works in the other direction as well. Their players tried to intimidate us. Nothing wrong with that. It's how the game was played. I learned early on that the kind of hit I hated the most was cross-checking. That's where someone comes after you with their stick held high, hands at both ends, and the middle of the stick directed hard and fast toward you.

It sounds like a dirty move, and it is. It is also technically illegal and should draw a penalty each time. The thing is, back in those days, refs rarely called a cross-checking penalty. Don't ask me why. They just didn't except in very rare circumstances.

If you went *too* hard they might call you, but that was not often. If you waited *too* long after the whistle, they would call you. But again, not too often.

I put two and two together pretty quickly and realized a couple of things. First, if I didn't like getting cross-checked, then it was a pretty good bet that opposing players didn't like it either. And second, if they weren't calling cross-checking penalties, then it was, for all practical purposes, legal.

The cost-benefit analysis I did at the time told me if I kept the severity and timing of cross-checking within certain parameters, I could get away with it.

Cross-checking *after* a whistle really worked. When the ref blew the whistle to stop play, guys stopped skating and let down their guard, and that was when I moved in and hit them with a cross-check.

This was an extremely effective intimidation technique. I used it throughout my career, and it served me well. But the thing to know is that it was not some random thing I did by chance. I learned the technique and the timing, learned how to get away with it, and I used it for all it was worth.

MIKE BOSSY FIGHT: WHAT WAS I THINKING?

MIKE BOSSY WAS A GOAL SCORER. WHAT DO I MEAN BY THAT? It wasn't just that he was not a fighter. Mike played ten seasons in the NHL for the New York Islanders, and in all but his very last season, he scored at least fifty goals. Nine years in a row. *That's* a goal scorer. The only reason he left the game was that he started having back problems and had to retire.

Being a consistent top goal scorer is no easy thing. Once opposing players know you can score, they start playing you closer, checking you more, getting in your face, doing whatever it takes to stop you. If you try to shoot every time you get the puck, they'll start playing you that way, and that will affect your ability to score. This means that besides having a good shot, you have to be able to make plays, get out in the open, pass the puck, and consistently receive passes.

Mike did all that and more. He could jump laterally and make it look like it was the most natural thing in the world. If he got a breakaway, you might as well let him go and have a relaxing cup of tea by the boards because you were never going to stop him from behind. He was that fast. A true superstar. That was Mike.

My first year with the Flyers, we were in New York, and the game was a little bit aggressive, with a lot of pushing and shoving on the ice. I got hit on the head with a stick a couple of times. That did not put me in a good mood.

Back then, when things got rough, when a fight was about to break out, every player found a player on the other team and grabbed and held them by the sweater. That way everyone was squared off with another guy, and there was no chance of a two-on-one situation.

I think a fight broke out, though I'm not sure anymore. Everyone went to grab the nearest opposing player, and for me that happened to be Mike. As I said, Mike was a fantastic player, but he was no fighter. Everyone knew it, and even Mike would tell you that.

Mike was a lot smaller than me, and I had my signature grip on him. I yanked on his sweater and arms, roughing him up a bit. As we were thus engaged, I thought, *If I fight Mike Bossy, I could maybe wipe him out in three or four seconds, and he would be too hurt to play. That would clearly improve our chance of winning the game.*

Was this another brilliant idea of mine? I'll let you decide as I tell the rest of the story.

While I had Bossy in my grip, trying to decide if I was going to fight him or not, Billy Smith, the Islanders' goalie, must have seen me yanking on Mike's sweater a little too hard for his taste, and he came out of his net, skated three-quarters of the way down the ice, and jumped on my back and took me down. He went all that way to protect his teammate, which, I have to say, I respected.

Billy Smith was a great goalie and a tough-as-nails player. Goalies generally don't get into fights. They stay out of that madness, but I guess me giving Mike a hard time was a step too far for Billy.

I never got a single punch in on Mike, but the next thing I knew I was down on the ice with piles of players on top of me. It might not have been a benches-clearing brawl, but it was pretty damn close. I was more or less trapped under there. My arms were pinned to my sides, and I was having a hard time catching a breath. Someone was choking me. I couldn't breathe.

I was desperate to get out of there. But how?

Let me take a small digression here. Back when I was fifteen and playing lacrosse, I got into a fight with a guy. I ended up on top of him, and he clearly lost the fight. Most guys would just take it. We'd get up, dust ourselves off, and finish the game. Not this asshole. He decided what he needed to do was bite my finger. Which he did. My baby finger. He clamped down on it so hard I thought he was going to bite it off.

That didn't happen, but that finger caused me excruciating pain for a few weeks, and it was very sore for about a month. Whenever I put my finger down after having it raised, the blood rushed in and the pain was immense.

Why am I telling you this? Because while I was on the ice under all those hockey players, I came up with another plan. As you may have noticed, back then I had a lot of plans. I figured I would do the same as that lacrosse player. I would bite the finger of the hand that was choking me. That would end the choking!

With great effort, I worked my arm out of the mess of players and pulled my hand away from my side. I slid it along the ice under the bodies of Islanders and Flyers. I was still not breathing, so I needed to get this operation going. When I got my hand up to my neck, I grabbed hold of one of the hands there and bit down hard on a finger.

When I say *hard*, I mean if I hadn't had my mouth guard in, I think I *would* have bitten his finger right off. I was desperate. I was getting choked, and this was all I could think to do about it.

That was when I heard a voice scream.

"Stop biting me! I'm the ref!"

Oh shit. I was chomping down on the referee's finger. Not good. The brawl broke up soon after that, and I was able to stand up and breathe again.

I probably should have been suspended for biting a game official. Why I wasn't, I don't know. My best guess is that the whole thing was so crazy that they just let it go.

So let's review. I tried to pick a fight for no reason with a non-fighter I greatly admired. *Check.* For my troubles I got jumped on by the goalie and ended up getting almost choked to death at the bottom of a pile of hockey players. *Check.* To get out of it, I almost got a long suspension from hockey for assaulting a game official. *Checkmate.*

All I can say is I love it when a good plan comes together.

MY SHOUT-OUT TO KEVIN MCCARTHY

When I was in junior, Doug Wilson, who you will recall gave me an injured hip that has lasted my whole life, told me about a defenseman named Kevin McCarthy who he said was unbelievably talented. A great skater, a hard worker, and a really good all-around player. Doug said, "The guy is up there," and he put his hand above his head. For him to say this really meant something to me since I looked up to Doug as an unbelievable player.

The Flyers drafted Kevin in the first round the year before me. When I came on in my rookie year, I saw for myself that Doug was right. Kevin played hard and skated harder. He was a great passer and smart. Basically, the guy could do everything.

He should have been on the ice at least as much as I was, probably more, but for some reason, he spent most of his time on the bench. During the season I averaged close to thirty minutes of ice time per game, and Kevin might have gotten a couple of minutes. This made absolutely no sense, but ice time is the coach's call, and in his wisdom he decided it was better to play me to exhaustion than to play Kevin. Go figure. I suppose it's like that old saying: some days you're the windshield, and some days you're the bug.

I remember one game against Montreal with Kevin sitting on the bench all of the first period and almost all of the second. With half a minute left in the second period, Bob put Kevin into the game. No idea what he was thinking in doing this, but okay, Kevin was going to get at least thirty seconds of playing time.

They set up for the face-off. Just before the puck dropped, Bob cupped his hands around his mouth and yelled out to Kevin, "Don't fuck it up!" That was just par for the course with Bob and his yelling, but I could see on Kevin's face that this particular yell from Bob hit him hard. And no wonder. That kind of thing is not helpful in that kind of situation.

The puck dropped. It bounced toward Kevin and took a crazy hop right over his stick. Montreal grabbed the puck and scored. The whole thing probably took just a few seconds. It definitely was not Kevin's fault. It was just colossal bad luck.

Kevin looked like he was going to explode. He finally got to play a shift, and Montreal scored on us. Incredibly demoralizing. So he pretty much remained on the bench for the rest of his time in Philadelphia.

Which is too bad. Kevin was a great player. He proved it the next year when the Flyers traded him to Vancouver. He got a lot of ice time there, quickly became their team captain, and went on to have several great years with that organization, even making the all-star team.

The point here is that you can be a great player, but you have to have a team that wants to play you. Otherwise you can't show what you have. I'm glad Kevin got to prove his skills when he left Philadelphia.

DEEP THOUGHTS 11

PLAYING HURT

I PLAYED FEW GAMES AT MY FULL STRENGTH. I HAD TO DEAL with allergies my whole playing career, and I also got various injuries over the years. I'm definitely not alone in this. Guys just played hurt or sick. Part of being a professional is that you give all you can give on every play in every game.

There were times I had an injured knee, which meant I was not as good at keeping guys from going around me on that side. Nevertheless, I did what I could. I gave all the effort and energy I had, and I did not complain.

Sometimes, when I was running low on gas because of how I was feeling, I would be out on the ice hoping the guy I was supposed to be intimidating did not clue in to my diminished energy and come after me. In those games, I held back from hitting too hard and hoped my history and reputation would keep him from coming after me. That usually worked.

At various times, players play games while hurt, sick, or whatever. Everyone was killing themselves trying to contribute. The team wanted you to play hurt and just "try your best." Then after a game of pain, we might get yelled at by the coach. "Why didn't you tell me you couldn't play?"

Why? Because that was the culture. No one ever said they couldn't play. No one wanted to be perceived as weak or unwilling to contribute. All of us were there to play and win, no matter what condition we were in. We all felt like it was up to the coach to pull us if he thought it was necessary. We sure weren't going to voluntarily give up ice time. No way.

Even with the allergies and the injuries, which caused diminished capacity, I consider myself a very lucky hockey player. I loved every second I was out on the ice, sizing up opponents, figuring strategy, and all the rest of it. I loved working with my defense partners when we were in sync, on the same page, making things happen. There was no better feeling.

I even loved practices. Working on my skills, getting better at skating or shooting or passing. The camaraderie with the guys on my team, all of us proud to do a good job out on the ice no matter the situation. Those were amazing times. It was great.

The average career in hockey is less than four years. Some players filled a temporary role, some got hurt, others lost the will to play or stay in shape. There were all kinds of reasons a career might end. My career was for 10 years and I could have played longer.

Was I ever too sick to fight? Was I ever too sick to play?

Yes and no. On the one hand, we were never too sick, injured, or tired to get out on the ice and play and try. That was a given.

On the other hand, there were times with my allergies, for example, when I just didn't have the energy to play a good game or get into a tough fight. Injuries took a toll on a player. Fights drained me of energy. Checks and hits and pests took a toll on you even when you knew and fully understood they were part of the game. Sometimes it was a struggle to get out on the ice for the pregame warmup.

I remember one time when we were playing Detroit, I was low on energy, and I got into a fight with Joe Paterson. At one point Joe went down on his knees. He had a hold of my sleeves. All I had to do was break his grip, and I'd be able to pound on him because he was in no position to fight. Easy. Except it wasn't. I didn't have any strength. I still think about this to this day. I *wanted* to break Joe's grip, but I couldn't.

Curt Fraser was on the bench watching all this unfold. I felt embarrassed that my friend Curt saw me weak like that.

Another time I got into a fight with Wendel Clark when he was with the Maple Leafs. Clark was their captain, a tough guy and a great player. The fight went okay, but I had no strength. I was just too sick and could not summon any strength or rage.

Those were times when it would have been best if I hadn't played or fought. Players saw me unable to break Paterson's grip and unable to put up a good fight against Clark. In other words, I was not intimidating.

That meant there were probably guys who figured I was easy pickings and went after me. For a fighter like me, that was dangerous. I had to be intimidating for my own protection. The more fierce I seemed, the less likely I was going to get hurt in a fight.

In cases like that, playing hurt or sick was not a smart thing to do. It showed grit and a willingness to contribute, but it also put me at risk.

THE HARDEST HIT OF MY CAREER

IN MY THIRD YEAR WITH THE FLYERS, WE WERE IN QUEBEC CITY playing the Nordiques in the playoffs. Their top line was composed of three brothers from Czechoslovakia: Marian, Peter, and Anton Stastny. These guys were fantastic players on one of the top-scoring lines in the NHL at that time.

All three were coming up on me and Bob Dailey, my defense partner for that shift. Anton had the puck in front of me, and as he crossed the blue line and began to cut to his left to make a play, I stuck with him and was tying him up a little.

This was a standard play, just like any other normal play. The forward comes at you, and you try to mess up their shooting or their passing. I didn't expect anything crazy to happen.

Then, out of nowhere, Bob, who was at least 250 pounds, cut over to blindside Anton with a hard hit. Not really sure how it happened, but somehow Bob missed Anton and ended up blindsiding me. Hard. Probably in the head, though I honestly couldn't tell for sure because I felt it through my whole body. He really shook me up bad. It was the hardest hit I took in my career.

I ended up flattened on the ice. Bob was out of the play as well after hitting me so hard, and Anton and his brothers went right past us and scored.

Amid all the cheering from the fans, I remember being so dizzy there on the ice that I could hardly tell down from up or right from left, and it took me a while to get my bearings. Bob hardly felt the blow. And why would he? He was stepping into the hit and was prepared for it, even though he did not hit the target he intended to hit.

The other thing I remember was being almost glad they scored. I was in no condition to play. There was some time between the goal and the faceoff as the officials retrieved the puck from our net and took it to center ice. That gave me some time to recover, though it wasn't nearly enough. I was concussed for sure. I managed to get up on my skates, and I remember holding my stick over my kneepads and leaning my head over, trying to figure out where the hell I was and hoping the dizziness would go away.

When I think about that hit, even today, more than forty years later, I still feel it: the dizziness, the intense disorientation for the rest of the game. Even the pain. It all comes back in a rush.

A lot of the tough events from my career are like that. Getting these stories out, reliving them and retelling them, one might expect would be cathartic, a way to get them out of my system and off my shoulders. Nope. They must be completely embedded in me because all the sensations from that time just come back as if I were still living them firsthand. Truth is, they are more like *Groundhog Day*. Every time I tell or write these stories, I relive them.

My second-hardest blow came when I was playing in Chicago. Look for my account of that stellar performance later in the book.

PAUL BAXTER: I NEVER LEARNED TO LIKE BEING SUCKER PUNCHED

THE PITTSBURGH PENGUINS WERE IN PHILADELPHIA, AND THEY were amped up, eager for a fight. I didn't know it at the time, but I guess they were tired of getting pushed around, and they wanted to stand up to us.

I had no quarrel with that. It was the game back then.

Paul Baxter played defense for the Penguins. I knew him as a tough player and an agitator, out there to cause trouble and intimidate his opponents. Gee, does that sound familiar?

At one point during the game, Kenny Linseman for the Flyers, a gifted agitator himself, caused some of his usual shit after the whistle, grabbing a guy and roughing him up a little. As usual, all the rest of us grabbed the nearest opposing player, and in my case that happened to be Paul Baxter.

To my mind, this was just a formality. I didn't think Paul and I were going to get into it. I was more interested in watching Kenny and his antics. I always enjoyed watching the shit that Kenny caused. All pretty funny.

Next thing I knew, I was down on the ice. Paul had sucker punched me. Not only was I down, but he had also loosened one of my teeth.

That tooth was loose for about twenty years, and it was sore for a good part of that.

This was at the beginning of the game. If I'd had any idea Paul was raring to deck me, I would have paid attention to him and not to Kenny. So after I hit the ice, Paul skated away like it was all over, but I was so mad at him for sucker punching me that I didn't want it to be over. I went after him, expecting a fight, but he dropped to the ice and curled up like a turtle, and I couldn't do anything to get him to stand up and fight.

With him in that position, I couldn't really hurt him, which made me even more mad.

Next season, we were playing Pittsburgh. The play was at their end. Paul was about a dozen feet in front of me, staking back to his end, but he wasn't skating very hard. More like gliding. Neither of us were anywhere near the puck or the play. I saw my chance, and I charged him and cross-checked him in the back of the neck.

He went down pretty quickly. He wouldn't get up, but I didn't know if I hurt him bad or if he was just stretching out the moment so the officials would notice and give me a penalty. As it turned out, that was exactly what happened. I got a five-minute penalty.

Pittsburgh scored three goals while I was in the penalty box. We were winning before that, but the three goals cost us the game. On two-minute penalties, you get out of the box when the other team scores. On five-minute penalties, that doesn't happen. So they just kept scoring while I sat in the penalty box. I got payback on Paul, which I was happy with, but no one there had to be a genius to figure out I lost the game for my team.

The coach was pretty angry with me. I broke the unwritten rule, which was that I was not supposed to do anything to protect myself.

If someone went after Bobby Clarke, I was allowed to go after them. I was an enforcer, after all. If someone took a stick to our goalie, I was allowed to hit them hard. I could take all the penalty minutes the officials cared to give out if it was in defense of my team.

But if I ever retaliated against someone who went after me? Well, that was a step too far. That was being a selfish player.

Let me say right here as clearly as I can: I never subscribed to that unwritten rule. In my mind, it was pure bullshit. If someone hurt me, I *had* to retaliate. If I didn't, I would be fair game, an easy target for any other agitator in the league, and my days in hockey would be numbered.

For some reason, no one else ever saw it that way. They expected me to take the hits and not fight back. I was not made that way.

Later in the book I'll tell you about another unwritten rule regarding face shields that I always considered just as wrong.

MY SHOUT-OUT TO MEL BRIDGMAN, THE FLEX MAN

I WAS FORTUNATE TO PLAY WITH MEL MY ROOKIE YEAR. HE HAD been on the team for a few years by then and was known as a tough, strong, smart center. Never afraid to get into a fight if he had to, and a really good player.

The first time I met Mel he was standing in the dressing room, and I would have sworn on a stack of NHL rulebooks that he was flexing his entire body. Mel had a spectacular physique, and his flexing looked over the top. I wondered why someone would do that? First, it must have taken a lot of energy to keep flexing like that, and second, who was he trying to impress and scare? His own team?

It's not too far from the truth to say he scared the hell out of me. I was careful not to look like I was staring at him too closely in case he got pissed off at me for staring. So I was really careful around him for the first month or so.

Then it hit me. Mel was not flexing. That was just his build. He had a lot of muscle, no fat, and he kept himself in phenomenal condition. Once I figured that out, we became pretty good friends. We lived near each other and carpooled to home games. Mel was a good player, and he had a long career. He was also thoughtful and considerate, especially to me when I was a rookie. He was one of those guys who always projected honor, integrity, and respect.

His work ethic was something else. During the offseason he attended classes at the University of Pennsylvania and got his undergrad degree. Then, when his hockey career was over, he went and got his MBA. Most hockey players don't get past eleventh grade. It's a tribute to Mel that he got his master's degree after two decades in hockey. It was a tremendous accomplishment, but that was Mel. Nothing held him back.

I was honored to have him as a friend. Mel was my role model on and off the ice, and I was even honored to have him in my wedding party when I got married.

THE DAY I TAUNTED WAYNE BABYCH

WAYNE PLAYED RIGHT WING FOR THE ST. LOUIS BLUES. I REMEMber him as a rugged player who skated well and had a great shot. Hell, he scored fifty goals one year. He was drafted three ahead of me in the same draft that brought me to Philadelphia.

During a game in St. Louis, there must have been a TV break or something because we were all standing around with nothing to do, waiting for the officials to start play again. I was on the ice with Mark Howe, and I don't know what got into me, but I said to Mark, "Listen to this."

I lined up next to Wayne and I started talking trash. I don't exactly remember what I said. With my mouthguard in, it was probably indecipherable. Which was probably good. Whatever I said, it would have been decidedly non-complimentary. They don't call it trash talk for nothing.

Mark started laughing, enjoying the scene. Since Mark was enjoying my taunts so much, I doubled down on them and just kept going at Wayne's expense.

I figured we were just having some good, clean fun. Well, maybe not *clean,* but still, fun. Pointless fun. When play finally resumed, the puck came across the ice between my legs, and Wayne charged after the puck. Or so I thought. Turned out, he wasn't after the puck. He was after *me.*

He put his stick between my skates, yanked it up hard, and hit me where it counts.

I was shocked. I had not played much in that game. Wayne had no reason to come after me. Except for the trash talk, of course, but that shouldn't have been enough for him to take a swipe at my nuts. But it was. He dropped his gloves and got the jump on me, and I was in another fight.

Wayne was a pretty big guy. I'm gonna guess he was six foot one and 195 pounds and a surprisingly skilled fighter. He had good balance and a good strategy, and he had more than a little bit of rage.

But he wasn't as big as me. Or as experienced a fighter as me. He really shouldn't have come after me. He shouldn't have been fighting in the heavyweight division.

But we were in it. I had a great grip on Wayne and felt confident he wouldn't be able to hit me, but he also had a pretty good grip on me. I started hitting Wayne hard. I began thinking he would go down soon and the fight would be over quickly. That didn't happen. To my shock and disbelief, he remained on his skates, and the fight continued, probably longer than it should have. Finally the refs pulled us apart.

A few days later, Keith Allen, the general manager of the Flyers at the time, summoned me into his office.

"Behn," he said, "the general manager over at St. Louis called and told me they thought you broke Wayne Babych's nose. But they were wrong! You broke his jaw and cheekbone."

I actually feel bad about what happened back then with Wayne and me. I have always had respect for Wayne as a player, and I suppose I shouldn't have taunted him like I did. He must have perceived it as a threat and acted accordingly.

He dropped his gloves and got into it with me, a guy he knew was a fighter. Anyone who drops their gloves like that is a winner in my book.

MY SHOUT-OUT TO CLARK GILLIES

CLARK WAS A LONGTIME LEFT WINGER FOR THE ISLANDERS, ONE of the great players who could do everything: skate, handle the puck, make great plays, and score goals. Part of the legendary Trottier-Bossy-Gillies line, he was a big part of why the Islanders won four cups in a row.

I remember him as big and strong, a tough opponent. A lot of times the tough players can slow down the play of skilled players, but that wasn't true of Clark. He was special that way. He kept up with Trottier and Bossy, and the three of them became the dominant line in the NHL for a lot of years.

One game my teammate Dave Hoyda got into a fight with Clark. Dave was a badass fighter, no question, but Clark was a premier fighter, and he won the fight against Dave pretty handily. You never like seeing your own guy get beaten, and what made it worse was how the Islanders' bench got really pumped up by the way Clark took Dave down.

I don't know what got into me, but for some reason I thought I needed to redeem our team. To be clear, I didn't exactly *want* to fight Clark. It was more that I felt like I had a duty to do so.

Fans who are at all familiar with my career might think it odd when I say I didn't want to fight Clark. The truth of the matter is no one could *want* to fight Clark. Period. He was a physical specimen, and his punches hit hard. If I got into it with him and made one mistake and loosened my grip on his punching hand, I could get my head smashed in.

Nothing happened in that game, but later in the season, we were playing in the Islanders. Clark and I squared off and dropped our gloves. I applied my signature move of holding down his right arm, and I got in some good punches.

Eventually Clark went down, not because I delivered a knockout punch but just because I hit him hard enough for him to lose his balance momentarily. In any case, that was a win for me. I avenged Dave. End of story, right?

Not so fast. After Clark went down, I did something I regret to this day. I raised my hand over my head and extended my index finger toward the roof in an "I'm number one" gesture. Why did I do this? Well, Clark was bigger than me, an absolute physical force of nature with the body of Adonis and the power of a boxer. And I beat him. Euphoria took over, and I did a victory gesture. It was a huge accomplishment to beat Clark the way I did.

Once I realized what I was doing, I immediately dropped my hand, but the damage was done. I felt like an asshole for disrespecting a great competitor like Clark in that way, and I'm hereby offering my sincere apologies to Clark for what I did.

Clark and I got into it one other time. He really fought me hard in that one, whacking me in my arm to prevent me from grabbing his elbow. I couldn't defend him from punching me, so he hit me lightly a few times. Eventually, I got a secure grip on his jersey at the right elbow. As usual, that was when my offense began. I got him with one good hit. It was a good punch, no question, but not enough to knock him down. Still, he *did* go down. I figure I must have knocked him off balance again. I got on top of him, and the refs immediately broke up the fight.

I have seen a video of an interview with Clark about our fights. His and my accounts differ greatly. The point we would both agree on, and the point I want to reemphasize is my strong belief that if you dropped your gloves, you won. It takes a lot of guts to drop them, no matter the situation and no matter your opponent. Any fight can lead to a lifelong injury. Clark was a hell of a competitor. Sadly, he's passed away now, and I want to remember him as the perfect combination of physical specimen and tremendous hockey player, and about as tough as they come.

DEEP THOUGHTS 12

FIGHTING VERSUS BOXING: THERE IS A DIFFERENCE

WHAT? ANOTHER DEEP THOUGHT ABOUT FIGHTING? GEEZ, Wilson, aren't you over it yet?

Well, what can I say? I was known as a fighter. I got into a lot of fights, so I have a lot to say about fighting. For example, this whole debate about the difference between boxing and fighting in hockey.

Some people seem to think there's an equivalence there. And at first glance, it kind of makes sense. Boxers pair off one on one, and so do hockey players. Boxers throw punches, and so do hockey players. But the resemblance ends there.

If I got into the ring with a boxer, I would not do well at all. I wouldn't expect to last more than a few seconds.

Boxers use their legs a lot. Their legs generate much of the power in their punches. They also bob and weave to evade getting punched themselves.

In hockey, you can't do that. You're wearing skates on slick ice. There isn't much anchoring to be done there. If you put too much leg into a punch, you're likely to throw yourself off balance. Also, there is no real bobbing and weaving because, again, you can't bounce on ice wearing skates. That's not how it works.

Another big difference is gloves. Boxers wear them. Hockey fighters drop them before the first punch is thrown. Boxing matches would be pretty short if not for boxing gloves. While gloves protect our hands, they are too bulky to punch efficiently. So we hit with bare fists, which takes a toll on your hands. Especially when you hit a helmet.

Another major difference is hockey does not have a bell. No starting bell and no ending bell. When does the fight start? When one of the players throws a punch? When someone's stick is whacked over your head? When someone jumps you from behind?

When does it end? When one of the players is too exhausted to go on, or when the officials break it up? Will the refs break it up quickly, or let you go?

Hockey fights involve refs. So what? They just break up fights when they get too viscous. Not exactly. Some guys use refs strategically. Say a smaller guy or a non-fighter is acting like he wants to fight with a fighter. Normally, this would be a mismatch and would rarely happen since the smaller guy would always lose.

But sometimes a smaller guy *will* get into it with a fighter, pushing and shoving the bigger guy, and wait for the ref to come between them to break up the fight. That's when the smaller guy throws a sucker punch over or around the ref to get the fighter. This is the only way smaller guys take on bigger guys. I saw this happen many times, and in my opinion, if the refs just let fighters fight, 75 percent of the fights would not even happen because the smaller guy wouldn't dare get into it with a bigger guy who could pound on him unhindered.

Of course, boxing doesn't allow this because they have weight classes. You don't put a heavyweight up against a lightweight. Not because the smaller guy isn't tough, but size and strength eventually get too hard to overcome.

Here's yet another difference between boxing and fighting in hockey. In boxing both fighters are fresh at the beginning of the bout, and they get tired at a more or less equal pace through the rest of the fight. You don't have a guy who has just boxed ten rounds go up against a guy who has not boxed a single round. That would be insane.

Well, hockey welcomed that insanity. Many times I would be at the end of a game where I was on the ice for half the game, and the opposing team would send out some goons to pick a fight with me. They were fresh as daisies. I was dead tired. Fair fight? I don't think so, but that was how it was.

Another crazy thing that happened was teams would bring up a player from the minors for just one game. Was that guy there to rack up goals and assists and play some good hockey? Not on your life. He was there to start a fight and maybe injure a guy enough that he couldn't play. Again, was that fair? My carefully reasoned opinion: hell *no*!

But it didn't matter. I had to fight the guy. I usually won, and he went back to the minors, only to be replaced by the next big hope who would come after me. It went like that in what seemed an endless loop. Rinse and repeat. It never ended, and it got old really fast.

My coaches left me out in these situations because they figured I could take care of myself. It was nice that they had such a high opinion of me, but I would have been okay if they'd put out a fresh guy against their fresh guys instead. Really, it would have been more than okay.

But maybe the biggest difference of all between boxing and hockey fighting is the purpose of the fight. In boxing it is to win the match. In hockey, winning can be a point of pride, but that is not the purpose. You engage in a hockey fight to unnerve and terrorize the other team. You are trying to throw them off their game by messing with their players. Once you have that in your head, you've figured out what hockey fighting is all about: intimidation.

MY SHOUT-OUT TO MARK HOWE: THE HUMBLE SUPERSTAR

WHEN I CAME INTO THE LEAGUE, I WAS SURE I WAS ONE OF THE fastest defenseman around. By build and musculature, I was no long-distance runner, but I was a sprinter.

Around my fifth year with the Flyers, Mark Howe joined our team, and I quickly got free tutorials on what true speed and endurance meant. He was faster than me, which came as a shock. But an even bigger shock was his endurance. Mark skated hard game after game, with many minutes of ice time, and never seemed to get tired. If you had asked me beforehand, I would have said such skating talent didn't exist. It couldn't. But it did. Mark had it. He was a skating freak.

I once asked him about his famous father, Gordie Howe, one of the great hockey legends of all time. He told me he used to skate with his dad and his dad's team, The Detroit Red Wings, when he was just fourteen years old. Pretty remarkable, but here's the kicker: even back then, when he was a young teen, he could keep up skating with an NHL team. Like I said, a skating freak.

Besides his skating, Mark had all the skills you could possibly want in a hockey player. He could handle the puck; he could pass; he could shoot. And he did it all with ease. He never won the James

Norris Memorial Trophy for best defenseman, even though I thought he deserved to win it with some of the great seasons he had.

My theory is that he made it all look *too* easy. He was so effortless in his superior play that no one thought he was doing anything difficult.

And on top of all that, Mark was just a great guy. A true gentleman. He was a superstar, but no matter who you were, if you were in Mark's presence, he made you feel like you were the star.

Once Mark joined our team, things changed for me. I went from averaging twenty-eight minutes of ice time per game to just a handful of minutes. I went from killing penalties and participating in power plays to essentially not playing at all.

I wasn't even allowed to practice with the team as a defenseman, which was bizarre in itself. When one of our defensemen got injured, I wasn't even put in their place. They called up a player from the minors.

As this new situation for me sunk in, I began to get concerned. While I was only twenty-four years old, I was not a kid anymore. Was my career effectively over? It usually is when you are sitting on the bench every game.

It was a precarious time for me, but I didn't sulk or whine or ask to be traded, even though I was boiling mad the entire season, terrified that my hockey story was over. Instead, I stayed professional, and I practiced hard. I kept in shape and worked on my skills so if I was ever called on to play, I could show I could still contribute.

That happened during a game when one of our guys got injured and I was tapped to fill in. I played a good game, was named star of the game, and I felt good about it. But next game I was back on the bench.

I asked Coach Bob what I could do to get back in the lineup.

"You should skate with Mark Howe during practice," he said.

I have always seen practice sessions as an audition. Each practice I tried to show the coach that I was worth putting on the ice in the next game. In this particular case, Coach Bob almost said it outright: practice with Mark. He basically set the terms of my audition.

He didn't have to tell me twice. I went and skated with Mark Howe.

Or I tried. I was out on the ice with Mark during his practice runs, and I was skating, but you couldn't say I was *with* Mark. Most guys in practice give about 80 percent. They don't go flat out. Mark was not like that. Every skating run up and down the rink, Mark gave 100 percent. He did not pull back even one ounce.

And there I was, always trailing behind him, always trying to catch him and never making it. Coach Cagey got some other guys on the team to come skate with me and Mark, figuring that would help get me up to speed to catch up with Mark.

That didn't work. They couldn't keep up with Mark either, and they quickly dropped out. Hell, they couldn't even keep up with *me*. They were getting ice time during games, so it wasn't so crucial for them. In my case, essentially sitting out the season, I wanted to show our coach I was in shape and could skate.

But Mark was just too fast. I went flat out. We passed everyone else on the team, but it was never enough. I left every one of those practices just beat, completely exhausted. But I was in shape, and if I ever got a chance to play, I would be in shape to play well.

As luck would have it, I never got the chance again in Philadelphia.

I also have Mark to thank for my dinner with a giant of the game, his dad, Gordie. We were on the road in Harford, and Mark said he was going to have dinner with his father and asked if I would like to come along.

Hell yes, I wanted to come along. I had played one game against Gordie back when I began with the Flyers. He was fifty years old and playing for the Hartford Whalers with Mark, and I was twenty. I knew of his reputation. Everyone did. He was a tough player, famous for getting his elbows in your face and his stick giving you trouble.

Before the game I was worried about taking him on. Did Gordie know about my elbows, my stick, my toughness? If I went after him, would I be accused of picking on an old man?

I asked Bobby Clarke about it.

"Don't worry," he said. "He's too old for that stuff now."

I wasn't convinced Bobby had that right.

During the game, Gordie came down the right wing into our end, and I was fixated on him. He was the legend. He was Gordie Howe, man. I couldn't let him get by me and score.

As I focused on Gordie, I made a big mistake leaving Mark out in the open in front of our net. Gordie passed the puck to Mark, who put it into the net for a goal. Ouch. I was so preoccupied and trying to get extra ready that I ended up paralyzed and did nothing.

All that was behind us the night the three of us had dinner. Gordie was just like his son: ultra humble and very generous in conversation. Both of them were superstars with incredible stats and amazing careers, but they never brought up any of that stuff. When you were with them, whoever you were, they both treated you with respect and were always very complimentary.

I still remember that dinner as a wonderful time with two wonderful guys.

MY SHOUT-OUT TO BARRY BECK

Barry played defense for the Colorado Rockies and the New York Rangers. But before that, he was an absolute terror in junior. Like Clark Gillies, Barry was a physical monster with a strong build and a well-deserved reputation for toughness.

Barry was also a defenseman, so we didn't get into much contact most games, which was fine by me. I did not relish the idea of fighting him.

As (bad) luck would have it, we were in Madison Square Garden one night taking on the Rangers. It was a chippy game, and some of the shoving kept going after the whistle blew on a play. I saw Paul Holmgren tied up with Beck. At the time, Paul had an injured rotator cuff. He couldn't raise one of his arms, which meant he would be fighting with only one hand. But Paul was tough as nails and was never one to back down from a fight. So despite this debilitating handicap, he was more than willing to take on Barry.

In a way it was none of my business, but I couldn't stand seeing this fight start with Paul at such a disadvantage that he could get seriously hurt. So I stepped in between them and grabbed Barry. I can't begin to guess what Barry was thinking, but he was as game to fight me as Paul was to fight him, and it didn't seem to matter that his opponent had been switched out.

I was fortunate that I got a grip on Barry's right elbow. We started exchanging punches. My grip held firm, and his punches did not land. Barry was even stronger than I expected. He had great balance, and he clearly knew how to fight. I fought back as hard as I could, knowing one slip-up and he could put his fist right through my skull. That was motivation enough for me to summon whatever rage I had.

In the normal course of our careers, we would never have gotten into a fight. Defensemen seldom interacted with defensemen, but in this case, I think I did the right thing by helping out my teammate.

Looking back, what were we thinking? We both were valuable players, and now about to kill each other. But we did it. We fought hard, and I'm offering my deep respect to Barry here.

DEEP THOUGHTS 13

HOW I REFINED MY FIGHTING TECHNIQUE OVER THE YEARS

I GUESS THE LESSON HERE IS ONCE I GET ON THE SUBJECT OF fighting, I'm not going to let it go.

I've said this elsewhere in the book, but it bears repeating because it is a fundamental principle and my unshakable opinion: *if you drop your gloves and fight, you are a winner.* Period. It doesn't matter the outcome of the fight. You came to mix it up, and that means you are a brave motherfucker, and as far as I'm concerned, you deserve all my respect.

One night in junior hockey, I got into a fight with Lynn Jorgenson of the Toronto Marlboros. He grabbed the inside of my elbow and locked his arm straight. I swung like crazy at him but to no effect because my forearm could not reach past his extended and locked arm that was anchored at my elbow. I didn't do any damage at all. I did almost all the swinging, but I didn't win.

This was a great lesson for me. I saw how tied up I was and instantly incorporated this technique into my game. Jorgenson's method worked. It was spectacularly effective, and I adopted it as the essential part of my fighting.

After that, for the balance of my junior career and all through my

NHL career, I started every fight by grabbing the guy's jersey at the elbow of his right arm. Then I locked my arm so it was straight out. Since my arm was longer than the distance from his elbow to his wrist, he really could not get a good punch on me. He might hit my upper arm, and if I had a poorer grip, I might get hit, but it wouldn't be a hard hit. If I didn't have that grip in place, I did not start punching. I worked to get that grip.

Once I had the grip secured, I started hitting. If my opponent was protecting his head, I hit his ear and the side of his head. That was pretty effective because at some point, as I was delivering a flurry of hits, he would inevitably raise his arm to protect his ears and head. That was when I would sneak in an uppercut, which was the hardest blow of all. Once I got an uppercut or two in, that was often the end of the fight.

I think you can probably see the one flaw with this method. What did I do when I was paired with a lefty? In that case, grabbing his right elbow would do me no good because it would leave his dominant hand free to punch me. And grabbing his left elbow would do me no good because it would just tie up *my* punching arm.

So what to do? That was when things got wild.

Neither of us would have any effective defense, so it would just become a punching match where we'd hit each other over and over again. Can you really win a fight one hundred punches to ninety-nine? That was what happened in my three fights with Terry O'Reilly. He was a lefty, which meant all our fights were brutal and long. All we could do was try to punch each other silly.

Training figured into playing and fighting as well. And your weight. You had to train for strength if you were to play the fight game. On the other hand, you wanted to keep your weight down to play the hockey game.

Most of my training was on the exercise bike because it built up the same muscles as the ones for skating. I would say 90 percent of my training that wasn't hockey skills training was on the exercise bike. The remaining 10 percent was lifting weights. I didn't want to overdo that because too much weight training puts on pounds, and that's detrimental to fast skating.

Every player had to decide what to do. I kept my weight at about 210 pounds throughout my career, and I carried a lot of ice time. To be my best as a fighter, I should have been closer to 220-plus pounds, but that would have taken away from my hockey game. I tried to be an all-around player, so I opted for the lighter weight. But the goal is not too heavy and not too light. Like Goldilocks.

Theoretically, that meant I was able to play both games: hockey and fighting. In practice, though, I felt like I came up short at both. I wasn't as good a fighter as I might have been if I'd had more weight and more upper-body strength. And at the same time, I was not as good a hockey player as I would have been if I'd been lighter and faster.

It was a constant battle between those two extremes, and I never really settled into one side of it. I wanted to be both a hockey player and a fighter, so I tried to stay in the middle for my career.

All this delicate balance went out the window during playoffs. I didn't want to risk too many penalties, which meant I didn't want to get into fights, and as far as I remember, I never did. So as we got closer to the playoffs I got my weight down to about 205 pounds. That got me into good shape for hockey, even though it made me more vulnerable as a fighter.

This wasn't a factor for the goons who went out on the ice for a few minutes of the game. They were not expected to play the entire game. They did not train to do so. They were focused on very few high-impact, high-energy minutes.

I always played a lot of minutes, so I kept my weight down. It meant I wasn't purely optimized for fighting.

RANDY HOLT: GIVE ME A BREAK

 going to say anything bad about any other player, and I really wanted to stick to that. As I've said many times, I played with and against so many great players. I was a very lucky guy.

In Scoop Malinowski's book about me, *Facing Behn Wilson,* he had an interview with Randy Holt. Randy decided to weigh in and make the conversation about himself. He said once during a game, after a whistle, Bobby Clarke had Randy's hands tied up, and Clarke told me to sucker punch a defenseless Randy.

Randy claims he threatened that if I hit him, he would come after me later, and because of that, I backed off, apparently too afraid of Randy's threat.

I bring something negative into my book only because this offended me. First of all, I don't remember any event remotely like this. I never sucker punched a restrained fighter. (I cross-checked, speared, hit from behind, and hit after the whistle, but I never sucker punched a defenseless guy.)

Now my objection to this is not because it sounds like I was afraid of Randy. Readers can form their own opinions about that. I take offense to the fact that Randy claims that Clarke would hold his arms and ask me to sucker punch him. Apart from being one of the greatest players ever, Clarke was tough as nails. He handed shit out, and he took shit. But he would never in a million years even think of asking a teammate to hit another guy like that. That just wasn't in Bobby.

KEITH MAGNUSON: CAN YOU BE SORRY YOU WON A FIGHT?

IF YOU'VE READ THIS FAR, I THINK YOU KNOW I CONSTANTLY tried to piss off and intimidate opposing players during the games I played. My stance is that was the way the game was played back then, and I was just contributing the best way I could.

Which brings me to my fight with Keith Magnuson. Keith had a long and solid career with the Chicago Blackhawks. When I played against him, he was the captain of his team, and he was winding down his career as I was just getting started.

We were playing the Blackhawks in Chicago, and it became a fairly typical rough game with a lot of pushing and shoving after the whistle. During one of those instances, we all grabbed the nearest player, and completely by chance—which was often how these things went—I grabbed Keith.

I applied my signature move where I grabbed the inside of his jersey at the elbow so he couldn't punch me. Believe it or not, I had no intention whatsoever of punching Keith. He had not roughed up any of my players and had not taken a cheap shot at me. I had no reason to fight him. Nevertheless, I was savvy enough to know I should protect myself after getting sucker punched by Tiger Williams.

Keith did not seem intimidated by me. He grabbed onto my jersey a hell of a lot stronger than I was grabbing his. This went on for a while as fights erupted around us. He kept pulling and yanking on my sweater. He was starting to piss me off.

We exchanged some words. I waved my hand in front of him and said, "Look," as a way of telling him to back off a little.

He must have interpreted that as "Let's go," because the next thing I knew, he started swinging. The fight was on and it went badly for him. I got a few good solid punches in, and he went down on the ice.

When the fight was over, an official escorted me to the penalty box, which was what I expected, and Bobby Clarke came over.

I was ready to receive some praise. I expected Bobby to tell me good job. I had a good fight, and I won. Congratulations. Or some such shit.

Instead, he said, in a decidedly derogatory tone, "What the hell are you doing?"

I sure didn't expect that. My teammate was disappointed in me because I won a fight? Bobby never questioned me on any other fight I ever got into, but he had something to say about this one.

I didn't know Keith very well. He was a good player, for sure, but I didn't know if he was a fighter or how big a fighter he was.

Never mind the fact that Keith threw the first punch. I never really knew exactly why Clarke was offended. Obviously, looking back after the fight, Keith was a tough, honorable guy, but not someone who should have tried to fight me, but he was too much of a competitor to back down.

His reaction did not make me change my way of playing, not for the rest of the game, and certainly not for the rest of my career. But it just showed me how different people can see the same thing in different ways.

It's kind of a funny thing that I won a fight and one of my own teammates was mad about it.

DEEP THOUGHTS 14

THINK YOU'RE TOUGH?

I'VE SAID BEFORE THAT IF YOU DROP YOUR GLOVES AND GET into a fight, then you are a winner, no question. However, picking a fight with someone who doesn't stand a chance against you does *not* make you tough.

So what makes a tough guy?

It all comes down to intimidation. If you can intimidate the opposition, and therefore diminish their playing abilities, then you are a tough guy.

Conversely, if you can take it from the opposition and *not* be intimidated, then you are also a tough guy.

Tough guys come in many flavors. There are the fighters, like me. There are the hitters. There are the pests, those guys who are always causing shit on the ice by hacking at you with their sticks or pushing and shoving all the time. All of those guys are tough guys because they intimidate the opposition. They keep the other guys from playing their best game.

Tough guys in these categories keep other guys from hanging out in front of the net where they have a good chance to score. Instead, those guys stay off to the side so they don't get hit or cross-checked. They got intimidated by a tough guy or a few tough guys.

If you can make a guy pass the puck sooner than he should have so he won't be a target of your hit, then you are the tough guy who intimidated him. Or, for an even better example, if you keep a guy from going into a corner after a puck, you have intimidated him because he's afraid to get roughed up. In that case, you are a tough guy who intimidated him.

Some of the great tough guys of this type from my playing years include Willi Plett, Terry O'Reilly, Barry Beck, Paul Holmgren, and Clark Gillies. These guys played a lot of ice time, which was intimidating in itself, and if you concentrated on their toughness, they would counter with great play and score goals. You couldn't get away from them.

Another category of tough guy is goal scorers. What? *Goal scorers* are tough guys? They sure are. Gretzky was no fighter, but he scored a million goals a season and another half million during the playoffs, and that was damn intimidating.

The great goal scorers had to be tough. They were always getting hacked at, hit hard, checked, and so on. But they did not get intimidated. You could not throw them off their game. They were laser focused on scoring, and no matter how hard you tried to push them off balance they never wavered. They just kept scoring.

Here I'm thinking of guys like Mike Bossy, Bryan Trottier, Bobby Clarke, Billy Barber, Denis Savard, Steve Larmer, Eddie Olczyk, and Troy Murray. All of these guys were great goal scorers, and they all had mental and physical toughness. You could not throw them off their game.

Paul Holmgren, my teammate in Philadelphia, was in a class by himself as far as toughness goes. He was not a super fighter, but he was tough as nails. He played like a wrecking ball, knocking guys down left and right. He was an unstoppable force. One year he had to get rotator cuff surgery near the start of the season, which would have meant he would have been out for most of the year. He put it off so he could finish out the season, and he still ran over guys like they were tissue paper. He was *never* intimidated by anyone.

I call that tough.

ARCHIE HENDERSON: WTF!

ARCHIE HENDERSON SPENT MOST OF HIS CAREER IN THE MINORS, where he had a reputation as a fighter. A big fighter. I think he led the league in penalty minutes for many seasons.

We were playing the Washington Capitals. Archie got called up for the game and—surprise!—actually started the game. Looking back, it shouldn't have been a surprise at all. He was a known fighter, and the Capitals were playing us, a tough team, so he was there to cause trouble. It didn't take him long to fulfill his duty.

Fifteen seconds into the game, the puck went into our end, and we started bringing it out to their end. I was skating up the ice following the play, and before I knew what was happening, I was down on the ice. Archie had two-handed a stick over my head.

That was completely uncalled for, and of course I could not let it go. The only problem was that I was pretty dazed, really in no condition to fight. If I got up in my addled condition, I would most likely get creamed in a fight with Archie since he was definitely *not* dazed.

The smart play was to stay down. What do you think I did?

Rage took over. I got up on my skates and locked up his right arm, which meant it was all offense for me after that. Despite being dazed, my rage served me well. I held him from punching me, and I got in many good hits to his face and head.

I'll give Archie this: he may have clubbed me with a cheap shot, but he was tough. I couldn't understand why he wasn't going down. How was he still standing? I thought I was giving him my best shots.

There is no doubt I won that fight. After we got separated, Archie skated over to me and said, just as cheerfully as you can imagine, "Good fight."

I was still mad at the guy. The way he clubbed me and took me down just filled me with rage. He should have been called on a major penalty for that, but—oops!—the officials missed it. So it was up to me to get even. Which I did.

And then he just casually came over and said, "Good fight"? What the hell was going on with this guy?

I learned later that this was his thing. After every fight he got into, win or lose, he would say the same thing to his opponent.

I didn't get it. It was very perplexing to me. You just took me down illegally, and now you want it to be like we're just a couple of gentlemen having a nice time out on the ice? No. That did not compute for me. My philosophy was if you tried to hurt me, then I was going to hurt you.

Later in the same game, Archie was coming up the ice toward our end. One of his guys was feeding a pass to him, but I anticipated the pass. I knew where it was going and raced over to Archie.

Now, normally in that situation, I would have given him a clean, hard check, which would have put the puck in play for us. But I couldn't let that stick over my head go. I came at Archie with my stick out intending to cross-check him in the face.

This was obviously a dirty move and a horrible thing to do. You can judge me for it, and I'm okay with that. Again, I didn't make the violence rules but I was sure as hell going to play by the same rules.

Once I got Archie with that cross-check, I figured he would be out cold, and I would have made my point.

That was not what happened. Instead, I somehow missed his head and ended up cross-checking him in the shoulder. That did not put him down, obviously, but it did get him extremely pissed off.

The rage took over both of us, and in a split second after that misdirected cross-check, we were at it again. I locked his arm, and the punches flew. Again, the fight went very well for me. And again, I couldn't understand how the guy was still standing. What would it take to put Archie down?

Years later, I heard from a guy who knew Archie, and Archie described this fight to him. "I was out cold on the ice," he said, "but I kept standing."

Now that's a guy I can respect. He could summon up the rage year after year. Being a longtime fighter is a tough way to go. Believe me. I know. But he did it. I heard he was a great teammate, and everyone loved him.

After he lost his two fights with me, he probably went back to the minors. I know he played the majority of his career there. He wasn't the first or the last player this happened to. Lots of teams installed minor league players for a game or two just to go after me. It was crazy, but that was the game.

I think their problem with me was that I played vicious and tough with everyone, including their top goal scorers. I didn't necessarily fight them, but I gave them a hard time. That made them think they needed to recruit fighters to take me on. It was another one of those unwritten rules: you don't harass the top players. But like I said, I didn't subscribe to unwritten rules.

Would I have preferred it otherwise? Would I have liked my time in hockey more if teams didn't bring goons in to cave in my head? Absolutely. But the pass-fail system was unrelenting. Archie failed and ended up back in the minors. I passed and kept playing in the NHL.

Maybe that's a kind of justice. I don't know. It's just the way it was.

MY SHOUT-OUT TO BRYAN TROTTIER

BRYAN PLAYED FOR THE ISLANDERS MOST OF HIS CAREER AND is one of the all-time greats of the game. He won a lot of Stanley Cups and just about every other honor hockey had to give. There wasn't anything Bryan couldn't do. He was a strong guy and very strong on his skates. The first time I met Bryan was at his home rink in New York. He was in the corner, corralling the puck, and I went after him from behind with a cross-check.

Up to that moment, I was not intimidated by Bryan. You could not be starstruck by the players you grew up admiring if you wanted to stay in the league. You had to treat them just like any other player. At least that was how I saw it.

I idolized Bryan as the great player he was, but for the duration of a game, he was just another opponent I had to deal with. Like I said, the league was pass-fail. Take care of business and contribute to the best of your ability, or get out. I went after Bryan hard. I expected my cross-check to knock him flying.

I moved him about an inch, maybe less. It was like a fly had run into him. I was shocked that my hit didn't do more damage.

In those days our two teams had the best lines in the league. For the Flyers we had Bobby Clarke, Billy Barber, and Reggie Leach. The Islanders had Bryan, Clark Gillies, and Mike Bossy. They were known as the Trio Grande. All six of these players were repeat all-stars. Both lines were phenomenal.

I often played on our line with Clarke, Leach, and Barber against Trottier's line. It was an honor to play with them. I remember after my first game against the Islanders, when I had been on the ice against Trottier's line, I was beyond exhausted. I said to Clarke, "I can't wait for Trottier to retire."

He looked at me. "How old do you think he is?"

"He's gotta be over thirty," I said.

Clarke laughed. "The guy's twenty-two years old," he said.

I think I reached another level of exhaustion at that moment, thinking about playing against Bryan for the rest of my career.

Which I did. Bryan was just an amazing player. I remember one game I was coming at him carrying the puck, and he was coming at me. I expected us to collide, but he did a move I was not expecting. He went down low so I went over him and cartwheeled in the air and onto the ice, much to my embarrassment.

Bryan wrote a book about his life and career a couple of years ago, *All Roads Home.* I read that book and loved it, and I called him up to congratulate him.

"There's one thing wrong with the book, though," I said.

"What's that?" he asked.

"You made yourself sound like you were a star, but you weren't. You were an absolute super-superstar."

He laughed, and we talked about how it was for both of us coming up in the league when we were just kids. How much we missed our families in those formative years. How much we hated being away from home, playing a tough adult game, a life-and-death game, basically as children.

I asked him if he remembered that time he sent me flying over him and I spun around like a pinwheel.

There was silence on the other end for a few seconds.

"Behn," he said, "I remember it like it was yesterday."

DINO CICCARELLI: BACKCHECKING? I DON'T NEED NO BACKCHECKING.

DINO HAD A LONG CAREER WITH SEVERAL DIFFERENT NHL teams. When I knew him, he was a forward for the Minnesota North Stars. Dino had this one trick that he played just about every game, and sometimes several times in a game.

Whenever we got the puck in our end and started up the ice to Minnesota's end, Dino sped up from behind me, got near me, and then fell down on the ice like I hit him with my stick.

I didn't touch him.

That didn't matter. He made like he was hurt, and the ref, who did not see what Dino was doing, assumed I had done something to Dino and assessed a roughing penalty against me.

There was nothing I could do about that. You couldn't tell the ref what really happened. It didn't work that way. Instead, I ended up in the penalty box, and Dino got a power play for his team without doing any of the hard work of backchecking. Sweet deal for him. Lousy deal for me.

I don't fault the guy. It worked for him, and soon other players were pulling the same fake move. It worked for some and didn't work for others. By the end of my career, lots of guys took dives and pretended they were hurt on the ice just to get the officials to call penalties on the other side. Hell, even Gretzky, when he wasn't busy scoring his two millionth goal, faked an injury with me.

If I could have gotten away with that tactic, I might have tried it myself. But I had what I guess you could call a moral code. I never let anyone think I was injured. No matter how hurt I was, I always tried to get up off the ice and back into the play or the fight or whatever was going on. It just wasn't in my blood to pretend I was hurt when I wasn't.

Maybe if I'd acted more like Dino...who knows? I used to wonder if Dino was laughing about all this. I don't wonder any more. I'm sure he laughed his ass off, and maybe he's still laughing today.

And you know, I could still be pissed off that his tactic worked on me so many times, but I have to admit, it's kind of funny what he got away with. So Dino gets my respect. Besides, if you can't laugh at yourself sometimes, what's the point?

JOHN HILWORTH: A PUNCH FROM THE PARKING LOT

JOHN'S CAREER WAS MOSTLY IN THE MINORS, THOUGH HE HAD a few stints with the Detroit Red Wings. John was a big guy, easily six and half feet tall, and he was a fighter, definitely full of the rage.

We were in Detroit one night, and John hit my partner, Jimmy Watson, way harder than necessary. As soon as that happened, I knew John and I were destined to fight it out because I wasn't going to stand for Jimmy getting hit like that. I took defending my teammates very seriously.

The face-off was at our end. They dropped the puck, and I was about ready to go after John right then, but it was a bad drop, and they had to do the face-off again. Before they could, Pete Peeters, our goaltender, called me over to the net.

"Behn," he said, "watch out for Hilworth. He's a lefty, and he'll throw a huge haymaker punch from the parking lot to start the fight."

"What?" I said. "How was I not informed that this guy was a lefty?"

Pete shrugged. Why didn't I get the message earlier? Pete knew him from junior hockey, so that was how he knew. And he saw that after John did a dirty on Jimmy, there was going to be trouble between me and John. Actually, I think everyone in the stadium—players, fans, coaches, refs, and maybe even whatever rats were in the walls—knew John and I were going to get into it.

I'm glad Pete told me when he did. If it had not been a false start on the puck drop, I might not have had the intel I needed to stand up to Hilworth. So thanks, Pete. Better late than never!

We set up for the puck drop again. It was a fair drop, and the play started. We ended up in the corner. Right on cue, just like Pete said, John tried to throw a haymaker at me.

But I had foreknowledge, knew it was coming, saw it coming, and tucked my head down so his punch just rattled off my helmet. If he had connected like he'd wanted to, he would have hurt me badly. No question.

Instead, I immediately countered with a right uppercut. I did not have time to grab his elbow like I usually did in a fight, but this time it didn't matter. His body went limp, and he fell to the ice. He must have been unconscious. I don't know for sure. I did know he wasn't fighting back, but I had the rage, and I just kept hitting him. I got in several punches before the refs pulled me off him.

Looking back, I feel bad that I might have been pummeling a guy who was unconscious, but in the moment, I didn't feel bad at all. I was playing the game the way it was played at that time. I have no doubt John would have done the same to me if he'd had the chance. He was a fighter, like me, and that was what we did.

ADIOS AMIGOS

FIVE YEARS INTO MY CAREER, I WAS STILL WITH THE FLYERS. I had gotten married the year before. We had a house in town, and the Flyers were my team.

Coach McCammon got promoted to general manager. As soon as that happened, I knew what was coming next. The general manager deals with acquiring and trading players. Bob had barely played me at all for a full season. I didn't have to be Sherlock Holmes to put the clues together and know he was going to trade me.

And trade me he did. To Chicago. The team had the right to do that without consulting me. Essentially, once you're on a team, they own your ass. They can play you or not play you. Keep you or trade you. They can do whatever they want, and there's little you can do about it. Except retire from hockey completely.

On the negative side, I wasn't getting any ice time in Philadelphia. To me, that meant they didn't want me. But on the plus side, a team wanted me, and therefore wanted to play me. Otherwise, why would they trade for me? When I went to Chicago, my playing time went back up to over twenty-five minutes a game.

The other good thing about that trade was that I had the summer to move. Sometimes players get traded in the middle of the season, and they have to hop on a plane that day to play for the new team the next day. In those cases, their family is left behind to figure out how to move to the new city, how to sell the old house, and all the other stuff that comes with moving. I at least got fair warning. My wife, Patti, was pregnant at that time, so having the summer to figure things out was a blessing.

I was five years into my professional career, and I was now a Blackhawk. Windy city, here we come.

PART 4

PLAYING FOR THE CHICAGO BLACKHAWKS

MY SHOUT-OUT TO KEITH BROWN: MY ALL-TIME HERO

A NEW TEAM MEANT NEW TEAMMATES. I WAS A FATHER NOW, with a young baby. Not a kid anymore. That was for sure. I was an adult with adult responsibilities. I had to make this work in Chicago.

I was very lucky early on when I got paired with Keith Brown on defense. Keith ended up with a long NHL career, much of it with the Blackhawks. I knew him as a wonderful friend and a rock-solid player. He was a fast skater and in phenomenal shape. He never seemed to get tired and never slowed down. Players tried to push him around, but they couldn't budge him. His skills as a defenseman were first rate. Forwards could not use speed to get around Keith. Keith was my defense partner for five years, and I don't think I ever saw him make a mistake in all that time. Hell, if Keith could be my partner, I would probably still be playing today.

He never coasted. His workouts on the exercise bike were legendary. He upped the settings on the bike so he was riding at a brutally high tension for close to an hour. I jumped in beside him and tried to keep up. The rides were outrageously tough. I could barely walk afterward. But being in great condition never hurt anyone. It was the effort to get there that was tough.

Just like when I was with the Flyers in Philadelphia and skated with Mark Howe, I skated with Keith almost every day. We raced up and down the ice. I say *raced*, but it was never really a race. Keith *always* won. I got pretty close, like maybe a yard behind, but he won every single race we had for five years. The guy was amazing.

The upshot is that I could never beat Keith at skating. But I had another option. Ever since I was a kid, I was pretty good at arm wrestling. I beat my older brother, even though he was stronger than me. In junior we arm wrestled sometimes, and I usually won. Even when I didn't, I sometimes lasted five minutes. I was a tough opponent.

So one night in our hotel room, I challenged Keith to an arm wrestling match. He was game. We got set up. I was bigger than Keith and figured I would win.

The first round, Keith put me down in less than a second.

That was, to say the least, shocking. Did that really happen? Yes, it really did. Maybe I wasn't prepared enough. That must have been it.

For the second round I got myself as prepared as I could be. I was focused. I took a deep breath, and I was ready.

He put me down in less than a second again.

The third round: same thing.

I don't know how many rounds we went, but I never lasted a second in any one of them. And Keith, nice guy that he is, kept telling me how good I was doing. Never mocked me or displayed anything approaching bad sportsmanship. Just encouraged me and let me know he appreciated my effort.

I swear, if Keith was still playing hockey today, I would come out of retirement to play with him. He's that good. He was definitely one of my hockey heroes.

CONCUSSIONS ARE GOOD LUCK

WE WERE PLAYING DETROIT, AND DWIGHT FOSTER WAS AGAINST the boards. As was my habit, I came in on him to hit him unnecessarily hard. He saw me coming, and at the last second, he ducked down and basically pulled my feet out from under me.

I had some momentum, and I went headfirst at top speed into the boards. So instead of taking Dwight out, I took myself out.

I was on the ice for a while, trying to get my bearings, trying to get the dizziness and the ringing in my head to stop. I didn't want to let on that I was hurt. That was not my way. But the trainer had to come out and guide me back to the bench once he got me up on my feet.

I had sustained a concussion. A pretty bad one because I remember very little of the next few hours—or of the next week, for that matter. Much of the story I'm going to tell I got from others who were there.

When I was back on the bench, the trainer asked me the usual questions.

"Are you okay?"

"Yes," I said.

"Are you able to take your next shift?"

"Yes."

"Do you want someone else to take your place?"

"Hell no."

Even in my dazed state, I gave the answers I was trained to give from all my years of playing hockey. They were burned into my brain. My father told me to never let anyone take my shift. My teammates also shrugged off every injury and said they were ready to play no matter what. I was so deep into the culture that I would never have given any other answers than the ones I gave to the trainer.

I did go out for a few more shifts. Some of the players went to the trainer and said I was not right. The trainer asked me again if I was okay.

"Fuck off," I said. "No one's taking my spot."

He walked away.

They said I asked my defense partner, Keith Brown, what the score was.

Now, the dizziness, the head ringing, the dazed look I must have projected, none of that alarmed anyone too much. But not knowing the score? *Every* player knows the score during a game. And besides, it's on a huge monitor right over center ice. You can't not know the score of a game unless you are completely out of it.

So that was a clue.

Next, I asked Keith, "Which way are we going?" In other words, I didn't know which end of the rink was ours and which end was Detroit's.

That was a step too far. Keith went to the coach and demanded that I be taken out of the game. They took me downstairs into the dressing room. Bob MacMillan was there. He hadn't dressed for the game. He sat with me.

"How's your wife doing?" he asked.

It sounds like a weird question, but it wasn't. Patti had had a baby earlier that day. Bob was just asking a natural question about someone who had just given birth. How was she doing?

The sad thing is, I did not remember her having a baby earlier that day. I just did not remember it. I said, "She's doing great. Her belly is way out to here." I put my hands out in front of me.

They took me to the hospital soon after that. The neurologist examined me.

"I'm going to say five things," he said. "Then I'm going to ask you in a little bit what the five things are."

"Okay," I said.

The first thing he said was apple. Then he said four more things. Then he asked me some questions, and we talked for a little bit. Then he said, "Tell me the five things I said earlier."

I could only remember apple. Nothing else. It didn't bother me that I was feeling lethargic, which happens with concussions, and I thought remembering apple was pretty good. Somehow, I knew I wasn't okay. But it didn't bother me.

I was in the hospital overnight. Then they sent me home. I don't remember any of that.

The next day, my mother, my daughter Ellie, and I were all getting ready to go to a different hospital to visit my wife and our new baby. As Ellie and my mom waited patiently, I would grab my coat, then think of something else and go into another room, then wonder what I was doing there and not come back. This sort of thing went on for some time, with me wandering from room to room, completely clueless. Somehow, I finally got it together enough for us to get going, but we didn't arrive at the hospital until nine,, which was after visiting hours, and we had to beg to be let in.

I remember later making some business calls. Then a week later, I called the same people and said the exact same things I said on the first calls. They said, "Behn, you talked about that last week." I didn't remember.

I went to the next practice, and the trainer was there.

"Did the doctor say you could play?" he asked.

"I don't know," I said. And I didn't. I had no clue.

"Did he say you could practice?"

"I don't know."

I don't know how many games I missed, but they finally dressed me. I sat on the bench feeling lethargic, but again, that didn't bother me. I don't know why they had me suit up. Maybe they thought I was an intimidation factor just by being there. My father always said the best seat in the house is on the team bench. He was right. I just sat there watching the game. Guys took what would normally be my shift, but for once, I didn't care. I was having a good time enjoying the game.

Toward the end of the game, we were on a power play, and the coach asked me if I was good to play.

Of course I said yes. What else was I going to say? You never let on that you can't play. Never.

So I went out on the ice. I was fresh. I had not cracked a sweat all night. That was for sure. But I was now on the power play. Almost immediately, the puck came to me in their end and I was all set up for a one-timer. That was what we called it when a puck came at you and you took a shot without stopping the puck. You got a little extra kick that way.

The problem with a one-timer is that it is hard to control where the puck goes. That was true for me that day. I shot the puck a good twenty feet wide of the net.

As luck would have it, and you can't control these things, the puck hit the shin of their defenseman and ricocheted almost ninety degrees and twenty feet into the net. I got a goal to go along with my concussion.

As usually happens after a goal, everyone came up and congratulated me, patted my shoulder or my helmet, and said things like "Great shot" and so on, but even in my addled state, even with my brain only half working, I knew that shot was colossally horrible. It was just dumb luck that it went in the net.

Okay. So far I'd played about ten seconds in the game. I guess the coach liked what I was doing because when I came back to the bench, he had me go out on the ice again.

Fine. There was only a minute or so left in the game, and we were up by one goal, so my job was to cross-check and hack at players, do everything I could to keep them off balance so they didn't tie the game. I did that for thirty seconds or so. Just working on pure instinct, I guess, because I was still foggy as hell. I was not exactly sure what was going on. Half the time, maybe even more than half, I didn't know where the puck was. Peripheral vision disappears when you have a concussion.

I went back to the bench. There was half a minute left in the game. Coach sent me out to continue hacking and crossing. I did that until the end of the game.

I played no more than a minute and a half in that game. I scored a goal, and everyone congratulated me on a great game—the players and also the coach. It was a truly shining moment.

I got over the concussion, and I don't have any lasting effects from it, at least none that I can remember.

I'm not going to say getting a concussion is a *good* thing, or good for your hockey career.

But on the other hand...

That one time, on that one day, it worked for me.

DEEP THOUGHTS 15

WAS I AFRAID? HELL YES!

WHAT WAS I AFRAID OF? YOU NAME IT.

First off, was I going to have a career? Lots of guys spent very little time in the league before they were out. Every practice was an audition for the next game. If the coach didn't like what he saw during practice, if you didn't hustle, if you didn't show mad skills, if you just coasted, well, that got you a first class ticket to the bench. Too many of those benchwarming games and you weren't long for the NHL.

Everyone, including myself, understood that you had to help win games or you'd lose your career. We all feared putting together a few bad games in a row.

Then there was the fear of physical injury. Was some guy going to put his fist through my skull or break my nose, cheek, or jaw? Was a stick going to blind me? Was I going to get blindsided or taken out from behind? Was I going to get cross-checked in the head? Was my own teammate going to take me out by mistake? All of these things were possibilities, and all were constant concerns to me.

Anyone who dropped their gloves with me had the opportunity to hurt me bad. On what planet would that *not* scare me?

One of my worst fears was playing a hard, long game, getting tired out at the end, and then having the opposing team send out a big goon who had been on the bench all night and was now fresh and ready to mix it up. A fresh fighter is a dangerous fighter, and he could hurt me.

I was hypervigilant about all these dire possibilities every minute of every game.

The one time I wasn't scared of any of these things was during my all-star game when I was with a bunch of great hockey players getting together and playing hockey. The fight game evaporated for those sixty minutes.

It was glorious, but fear is a funny thing. I did not have to worry about getting mauled or receiving a career-ending injury in that game, which meant I didn't even have to smear Vaseline on my face. No one was going to punch me.

Except I was so used to it, I did it anyway. I smeared Vaseline on my cheeks, chin, nose, and forehead.

Sometimes fear habits are hard to break.

MY SHOUT-OUT TO DENIS SAVARD

KEITH WAS NOT THE ONLY GREAT PLAYER I KNEW WHEN I WAS in Chicago. Denis Savard played center mostly with the Blackhawks but also had a few seasons with Montreal and Tampa Bay.

I've already talked about Denis earlier in this book, but he deserves a shout-out of his own, so here it is.

Denis could go from a standing start to top speed in one stride. It was a remarkable thing to see. He could handle the puck and was always a threat to score. The guy had thirty goals or more just about every season he played. He was a great passer too. While everyone was worried about Denis and tried to keep him caged in as much as they could, he passed to Steve Larmer, another fantastic player who also had a great shot and who I'll get to later.

Denis was famous for turning nothing plays into goals, and he often did it with a move everyone called the spin-o-rama. He'd come up on a player, one-on-one, and then, out of the blue, execute a circular move on his skates where he went backward for a split second, hauled the puck around in an arc with his stick, and got by the opposing player to get a shot on goal.

Whenever I saw this move of Denis's, I wondered how the hell anyone could do that. I never saw anyone else who could. They didn't have the nimbleness to pull it off. If I'd ever tried a move like that, I would have been tied up by the defense before I got halfway through a spin-o-rama.

Not Denis. He knew how to make it work, and he did, scoring electrifying goals off his spin-o-ramas that fans loved to see. They went absolutely wild whenever they saw it, and I don't blame them. It was a beautiful thing to see.

Even more remarkable is that I never saw Denis rehearse this move in practice. He deployed it when needed in a game as though it was just normal. Like everything else he did, he made the spin-o-rama look easy.

A GAME AND A BRAWL AGAINST TORONTO

During one of my first few years with Chicago, we were playing Toronto, and we were beating them by four or five goals with thirty seconds left in the game. The rational thing to do, for both teams, would have been to ride out the clock. The game was over. No team scores four goals in thirty seconds.

But lo and behold, Toronto didn't want to let things end so easily. They put all their toughest guys out on the ice for that last half minute. Some were defensemen who were put out on forward. Something defensemen don't do except on very rare occasions. Why would they do that? Because they were setting up for a completely different game.

The message Toronto was sending with that deployment of fighters was very clear. We weren't going to be playing hockey anymore. We were going to be playing the second game, the fighting game. They wanted to show they could take us down physically.

My feeling was that we had to do the same. If they were going to deploy force, we should too. Only problem was, our coach didn't see it that way. He left Denis Savard out on the ice. To me, this made absolutely no sense. As I've said, Denis was one of the top players in the league. He was a phenomenal goal scorer, and we needed him to do exactly that.

But we didn't need him to get into a fight against fighters. There was no question that we were going to win the game. Leaving him out on the ice in a brawl left him open to getting an injury that could put him out of commission for several games or even for the rest of the season.

And the thing is, we had plenty of tough players on our team. We could meet Toronto head on and give them a run for their money.

We had a TV break before the puck was to be dropped. I skated over to our bench and had a loud conversation with Curt Fraser.

"I kinda think Denis should sit the rest of the game out," I said.

Curt picked up on what I was doing. "Yeah," he said more loudly than necessary for me to hear him. "Guy deserves a little rest after the game he put in."

I glanced over at the coach. He didn't seem to notice our conversation. He also didn't seem to get that leaving Denis on the ice was a dangerous thing to do to Denis and to the team.

"It is going to get ugly out there," I said.

"For sure," said Curt. "I'm good to go."

We both looked toward the coach. He was not picking up on what we were saying. I didn't know what else to do. Player deployment was the coach's responsibility.

The TV break ended. Curt and I exchanged shrugs, and I went to set up for the faceoff. Before the puck was dropped I had a few words with Keith Brown, my defense partner.

"There's no sense in playing the puck," I said. "Do not look at the puck. They're going to come at us as hard as they can with their sticks to our heads to start a fight."

Keith nodded, but I'm not sure he understood because when play started, the puck went into his corner, and Keith went after it, like anyone would normally do when the hockey game was on. Only the hockey game was not on anymore. We were in the other game. The fight game.

A Toronto player came up from behind Keith and hit him hard in the head, which was exactly what I thought would happen. Keith is a big guy, and I knew he could take it, but that wasn't the point. By the unwritten but well understood rules of the fight game, I could not let that pass. I came up behind the guy who hit Keith and ran over him exactly how he had run over Keith.

Once that happened, the brawl was on. Everyone dropped their gloves and paired off, and the punches started flying. One more time I had to summon up the rage for a fight, this time at the end of a game when I was tired and the game was already determined.

I paired off with Bob McGill. He was a good fighter, but I outweighed him by quite a bit, and he really didn't have a chance against me.

Other fights were going on around me, but as usual, I had a good grip on Bob's arm, and the fight was mostly about my offense. Toronto started this, so I didn't feel bad about beating Bob. Bob later became a teammate, and he was, and is, a great guy. Nothing here was personal. The Toronto coach was pissed that his team had lost by so much, and he decided this was how he wanted to end the game. If he couldn't beat us in hockey, he was going to try to beat us in fighting.

To be clear, this was not some new tactic Toronto's coach came up with. This sort of thing often happened in lopsided games.

I've pointed out a few times in these pages where I thought some things were just batshit crazy back then. This is a perfect example. It made no sense to have a brawl when the game was settled, but it happened far too often.

I'm not sure how Denis did in the brawl, but he was not injured and played the next game just fine, so all was good there. Still, it was a risky thing to leave him out there when a brawl was sure to break out.

What were we thinking?

MY SHOUT-OUT TO STEVE LARMER

STEVE WAS ANOTHER LONGTIME BLACKHAWK. HE PLAYED RIGHT wing with Denis Savard.

When I was on the bench during my career, I saw that time as an opportunity to learn. I watched the players on the ice, guys on my team and guys on the other team, and I tried to steal moves or tricks or figure out how they did things.

Steve had a knack for getting out in the open to receive a pass from Denis or another player. He had a great shot and scored a lot of goals that way. He did this again and again, and I could not figure out how he did it because a lot of the time he went somewhere on the ice that I did not expect. Someplace no one would think he should go.

So after one of these games, I went to Steve and asked him.

"Steve," I said, "the play was in the corner, but you went on the other side of the net, which made no sense to me or anyone else watching. Why did you do that?"

Steven was a pretty humble guy, not one to brag about his abilities. "Yeah," he said. "I guess I messed up."

"No, no, no," I said. "You scored a goal. You can't call it messing up if you scored. But the move was counterintuitive. What made you do it?"

Steven didn't have an answer for me. I suspect it all came down to natural talent. It wasn't luck. This wasn't a one-time thing where he got into the open to receive a pass. He did it game after game after game. It was one of those things I tried to do but couldn't, at least not at the level Steve was able to execute.

Natural talent only takes you so far. You still have to work at your skills, which Denis and Steve definitely did. But Denis also had the spin-o-rama and Steve had a knack for getting in the open. They worked beautifully together and won a lot of games for us. They were something to see.

RITUALS REDUX

I TALKED ABOUT PREGAME RITUALS EARLIER, BUT I WANT TO talk a little more about sticks. A lot of guys were close to obsessive about their sticks, including me. We all had strong preferences about the thickness of the stick, the length of the stick, the lie of it on the ice, whether the curve was closer to the heel or closer to the toe, and on and on. A stick was a very personal thing. And maybe the *most* personal thing was how we taped our sticks.

Did we tape them with white tape or black tape? How much tape did we use? Was it a few loops or several loops to cover most of the blade? Was the tape closer to the heel of the stick or to the toe of the stick? How much overlap on the loops did we want with the tape? And so on.

Some of this was to make our sticks suited to our style of play, whatever that was for any particular player. But some of it, I'm convinced, was just part of the pregame ritual. We spent time taping up four of our sticks before each game so we had reserves in case of breaks, and this taping became a ritual for a lot of guys.

When I was in Chicago, one year my defense partner was Gary Nylund. A great player, a great guy, and a really good friend. We lived not too far from each other, and one night he asked me to pick him up the next day and take him to the game.

I said, "Sure, no problem," and then the next day I got in my car and drove to the arena, and I completely forgot to pick Gary up. When I say completely, I mean I didn't even realize he was not in the dressing room as I was humming a tune to myself and carefully taping up my sticks just perfect for the game. I was so into the ritual of taping that I was completely clued out about Gary's non-presence.

That was when we got a call in the dressing room. I picked up the phone. "Behn," said Gary on the other end of the line, "where are you?"

The blood drained from my face. I felt horrible. How could I have forgotten my teammate and defense partner like that?

I was panicked and frantic because coming late to a game is a big no-no. Management hates it, and it reflects badly on the player. It makes you look like you don't care, you're not a team player, or you don't have drive.

I told Gary to hang tight, and then I called my wife, Patti, who was at home with three kids under the age of three, and asked her to please get the kids into our other car and go pick up Gary and bring him to the arena. That was going to be a lot faster than me driving all the way back.

She did it, and I was so thankful to her. Still am. That was a great thing to do.

Then I had to go tell the coach what happened.

I went into his office and started talking right away. "Gary being late to the game is completely my fault," I said. "One hundred percent on me. I'm the idiot. I didn't pick him up at home like I said I would. Don't punish Gary for my screwup."

Coach just nodded his head. Maybe he even laughed. I don't remember, but I protected Gary's reputation as best I could.

Then I went back into the dressing room, and I found one of Gary's sticks. Even with my wife picking him up, he was going to be too late to tape his own sticks. I had to tape them for him. I studied that stick like I was cramming for the most important exam of my life. I saw how he looped the tape. I saw where he placed the tape on the blade and noted how much overlap he put on the loops. I was ready.

I got four of his sticks out and taped each one precisely the same way as the stick he taped.

Gary made it to the arena and came into the dressing room.

I was apologetic as hell. "Sorry, Gary," I said. "I don't know what happened there. Just forgot. I'm an idiot."

"Don't worry about it," he said.

He was good about it, but we were both upset. I screwed up, and he was late. I showed him the sticks I taped. "Thanks, Behn," he said as he examined each one. "These are perfect."

That felt better. At least I got his sticks right for him.

We went out for a short warmup before the game. Gary was using one of the sticks I taped for him in *exactly* the same way he taped his sticks. Or so I thought.

Right after warmups, Gary was in the dressing room taping up four sticks. The ones I did for him were not so perfect after all.

I never asked him what was wrong with the ones I did, but it just goes to show how personal something like tape on a stick can be. Maybe I really screwed up, or maybe he needed the ritual, but the bottom line is no one can duplicate how you tape up a stick, no matter how hard they try. No one can replace that ritual.

THE SECOND-HARDEST BLOW OF MY CAREER

I SELDOM TRIED TO CHECK OR HIT ANYONE MID-ICE. THERE was too much chance of missing my opponent and him getting around me with a chance to score. I much preferred getting my guy against the boards or, better yet, in the corner where I could tie him up or cross-check him. Besides, cross-checking was more intimidating and hurt more than body checks.

Looking back, I should have stuck to that principle.

I don't remember the game where this happened, but I do remember Keith Brown, my defense partner in Chicago at the time, had a guy tied up mid-ice, angling him toward me.

Well. I thought this was my chance. I decided to take a run at this guy Keith had discombobulated, at the same time thinking how proud I was of myself for being about to log my first open-ice hit in years.

So I went in hard, kind of like how Bob Dailey went in hard on Anton Stastny a few years earlier. I told that story in Part 3. I don't know exactly what happened, but somehow I never got to apply my hit. Instead, his stick hit *me*. With me moving in fast, the spear of his stick went through my lower lip and rattled my teeth. Technically, I probably didn't even hit him. I may have brushed past him, but I certainly didn't detain him.

He yanked his stick back, and I ended up with a nasty, bloody tear clear through my lower lip that required a dozen stitches on the outside and almost as many on the inside. My teeth were sore for a long time after that.

My great play turned out to be a pretty bad injury for me. Of course, in those days, stitches didn't keep you from playing. Hell, I could have had a broken arm, and I would have said I was good to play and the trainer and the coach would have said, "Okay, sounds good."

So I played with all those stitches. Funny thing, I had to get a procedure done a few weeks ago that required a few stitches, and the doctor gave me all these instructions. "Don't exercise for two weeks. Don't exert yourself." Don't do this. Don't do that.

Now just when exactly did the rules change? Because I did not notice when that happened. I thought it was still like it was back in the day, when stitches essentially meant nothing.

Stitches were nothing new, of course. I had been cut many times in my career. I actually remember early on, I was getting so many stitches that I worried no one was going to want to look at me, let alone marry me. I thought maybe I needed to get married quickly, before I looked like Frankenstein with all the stitching all over my face.

What made this particular time, with those dozen stitches on my lower lip, even worse was that by then we had our first daughter, Elizabeth, waiting at home for me. Nothing felt better than lifting her up after a night of hockey, holding her close, and hugging her. But I started to wonder how much she was going to like it if her father kept coming home with stitches all over his face. That row on my lower lip was pretty startling and must have been scary for a young child.

Those thoughts were the first inkling of my starting to see a life after hockey. I was beginning to see that my family was more important than the game, and I needed to think about what that meant going forward.

So the second-hardest blow of my career was also something of a wake-up call that I would have to answer soon enough.

MY SHOUT-OUTS TO TROY MURRAY, EDDIE OLCZYK, AND CURT FRASER

TROY AND EDDIE, WITH CURT, WERE OUR SECOND OFFENSIVE line when I played for Chicago. They went out on the ice when Denis and Steve's line was between shifts. But they were just as good as any first line.

Troy played center, which is a tough position to play. You are expected to play offense, making goals happen, but when the play is in our end, centers are also expected to pitch in on defense. That means a whole hell of a lot of skating. First going up the ice to try to score, and then also being quick in our own end to help stop the other team from scoring.

It's a lot of skating, a lot of hustle, and it can be exhausting to play center. I couldn't do it, but Troy made it look easy. He was truly amazing. Just like Steve Larmer, Troy was a humble guy and never bragged about his abilities. He was a dedicated player.

One season Troy was on his way to scoring fifty goals. That was always a great milestone for a player. Troy was at about forty-five with about fifteen games to go in the regular season. He was well on his way. It was in his grasp, and we were all rooting for him to make it.

Then one game he got hit hard or he was cross-checked. I don't remember exactly what happened, but he broke some ribs. Broken ribs are no picnic. They can hurt like hell, and there isn't much you can do to fix them. They just have to heal on their own. Troy didn't let any of that stop him from trying to reach that magic fifty. He kept playing the rest of the season. I don't think he missed a single game, but unfortunately, he didn't get to fifty, which was too bad. He had a great year, and it would have been nice for him.

One of his partners was a relative newcomer, a young guy named Eddie Olczyk. He came into the league as a strong skater and a good scorer. He was a huge addition to the team and helped us take two games from the Edmonton Oilers in the playoffs. This was when they had Gretzky, who at the time was poised to get his three millionth goal.

Terry, Eddie, and Curt Fraser did excellent work against Edmonton. No other team that year took two games from Edmonton in the playoffs, and a big part of the reason we did was that we had Eddie there in the second line. We were able to make Edmonton work for their wins.

Which brings me to Curt Fraser, the third member of the line. Curt played for the Vancouver Canucks when I first came into the NHL. I was with Philadelphia then, and before one of the games with Vancouver, I went over Curt's sheet, just like I would with any player. I wanted to know if he was scoring, if he was a passer, and if he racked up a lot of penalty minutes. Was he a fighter, or wasn't he? No sense finding out any of that stuff for the first time when you were out on the ice.

I did notice that Curt had a lot of penalty minutes on his sheet. In my book, that tagged him as a fighter. Most of the guys, when I asked them about other players, would say, "Oh, don't worry about him, Behn. You can take him."

That wasn't the case with Curt. Before the game, Mel Bridgman said something like, "Behn, you need to worry about Curt."

Well, I didn't want to hear that. Where was "Don't worry about him, Behn"? Where did that go? I worried enough on my own. I didn't need any encouragement. Not that I wasn't glad for Mel's heads-up. I was. I just didn't want it to be true that I needed to be careful of Curt.

The game got started. After a whistle blew, I took the opportunity to get in a cross-check on one of the Canucks, which was my habit. Curt didn't like that and was having none of it. He immediately dropped his gloves, and we were in a fight.

I soon learned why Mel warned me about him. Curt was exceptionally strong, and he had the rage. He knew how to fight. It looked terrifying. We exchanged some brutal punches, but they didn't quite land because we each had a good grip on each other. The fight went on for a while, and I felt like I was always a split second away from getting my skull cracked open.

As I look back, I can honestly say this was a great fight. We were two seasoned warriors who knew what we were doing, and we took care of business. All my other fights, if I had to assess them, I would have to say they were stupid. Pointless and dangerous. Not this one.

We eventually got separated by the linesmen. Neither of us was hurt, but we had both been in a fight, and we knew it. I had great respect for Curt. He dropped his gloves, came after me hard, and took as much as he gave. He was a winner as far as I was concerned.

None of this meant neither of us was pissed at that moment. I know he was because I cross-checked his teammate, and he didn't like it. I know I was because we were in a fight, and in a fight you don't let respect get in the way. You are there to pound on the other guy. Rage takes over, and there's no stopping it.

We were trying to hurt each other. Make no mistake. Every fight I was in, I was trying to hurt the other guy, and I'm 99 percent sure the other guy felt the same. You really do feel like you're fighting for your life, and the only thing keeping you alive is the rage that gives you extra strength to land punches.

The rage is important. You can't just hope it comes. You have to summon it up at the speed of light to match the rage in the other guy. These fights last about thirty seconds, sometimes a minute. You don't have time to warm up. You have to be ready to go. The rage has to be there, in reserve and primed for action.

Now, off the ice, it's a different matter altogether. We can talk about things, be friends, even laugh about things. That's a whole other realm. On the ice, it's a battle.

Later, Curt and I both ended up on the Blackhawks, and we became great friends. Why wouldn't we? Curt is a great guy. A lot of fun to be around. Our fight, the one where I thought I might have my head kicked in, was old news by then.

Curt never looked for a fight, but if one came to him, he wasn't afraid of anyone. He brought it to his opponent with energy and skill. I was glad when he and I were playing on the same team. Not only did he really help the line that included Troy and Eddie, but it meant I never had to fight him again.

BOB PULFORD, A.K.A. DR. BOB

LET'S LEAVE ALL THOSE GREAT GUYS I GOT TO PLAY HOCKEY with for a moment and let's talk about Dr. Bob.

First thing to know: he was not a doctor. That was just what we called him. Bob had a long playing career mostly with the Toronto Maple Leafs. After that he went into coaching, and when I was on the Blackhawks, he was our general manager.

Bob commanded a lot of respect from his players. We feared him and we loved him. No one wanted to let Bob down. He had that effect on people, and I guess you could call that a gift.

When you got hurt, no matter what your injury, Bob had you come into the training room three times a day. Each of these times he had you get in a very hot tub for about twenty minutes. Then he had you get in a tub of ice water. Three times a day he had you go through this regimen, and it was terrifying and awful. We all hated it. No one could like it. It was painful. You had to come in early for the first session and stay late for the third session. This torture went on for days.

I don't know if it helped anyone's injury. It might have, but I think for me, whatever injury I had would probably have improved without the boil and freeze.

Once your injury *did* start to improve, Bob got you skating. He put on his own skates and went out on the ice with a folding chair and set it up somewhere in the middle of the rink. He always wore a suit, so he took off his blazer and draped it over the chair. In his shirt and tie, he sat down in the chair and put a couple of packs of cigarettes next to him on the ice with a lighter on top of them.

The clear signal, when I saw Bob all settled in, was that I was going to be skating for a long time.

And I was not wrong. Bob had us do full-length shooting drills where you skated the length of the ice. You could carry the puck and shoot or lose the puck but keep skating anyway. Then you went the length of the ice the other way and did the same. We did this with Bob over and over and over. Sometimes I was by myself; other times, if there were other injured guys, we did the drills together.

After doing this endlessly, run after run after run, we got so sick that we threw up over the boards. Did that give us an excuse to stop? Absolutely not. After we puked, Dr. Bob had us back doing skating drills.

Then we did the hot tub and the ice tub, grabbed a bite to eat, and went back on the ice and did more drills. Not sure getting lunch was worth it, since we got so exhausted that we might throw up again.

I was under no illusions as to what Dr. Bob was doing. He was torturing us so we would get to play sooner. No one liked these drills. They were awful, and it seemed like they would never end.

I will say one thing, though. He got us back into game shape quicker than we might have otherwise. Besides that, no one was going to defy Bob and tell him they weren't going to do these drills. No one would even think of such a thing. We had all kinds of respect for him and did whatever he asked us to do.

This sort of thing, where Bob got involved with rehab, was not even the normal duty of a general manager. They usually dealt with players, trades, contracts, and that sort of thing. In most cases, when you got injured, a trainer helped you figure out what therapy you needed to get past the injury and was very careful about when you should be skating again.

Bob wanted his players on the ice and playing in games as soon as humanly possible, so he took it on himself to make sure that happened.

It was torture, no question about it, but it worked. I wanted to get into playing shape so I wouldn't have to endure his treatments or his drills.

DAVID LETTERMAN RECOGNIZES MY GENIUS AND GIVES ME FIFTEEN SECONDS OF FAME

WE WERE IN NEW YORK PLAYING THE RANGERS. I WAS TAKING the puck out of my end. All our forwards were heading up the ice to the Rangers' half of the rink.

What I did next happens in every hockey game many, many times. There was no point in trying to finesse the puck over the blue line because New York had all their guys there. What usually happens in a case like that is the defenseman (that's me) crosses center ice and fires the puck into the opposing end so it hits the boards or the glass about halfway between the blue line and the goal.

Then the puck rattles around the corner and heads behind the net. The goalie usually comes out of the net to trap the puck and try to pass it to one of his guys. While he's doing that, our guys go in and try to get the puck away from him or try to block his pass. All this is a basic play that happens dozens of times in a game.

Every Blackhawk and every Ranger knew exactly what was coming. Except this time things did not happen the way they usually did. I slapped the puck high so it hit the glass. I fully expected it to continue around the corner. So did everyone else on the ice, including the goalie. He came out of the net and positioned himself in the normal place behind his net to intercept the puck.

Only the puck never got to him. It hit one of the metal braces between the panes of glass and took a ninety-degree turn and began heading toward the net.

At first, no one knew where the puck was because no one expected it to do that. I had never seen a puck ricochet like that and have never seen it since. It was a once-in-a-lifetime freak bounce.

By the time the goalie realized what was happening, it was too late. He couldn't get back in front of the net in time to stop it, and the puck crept into the empty net for a goal.

I scored over one hundred goals in my career, and this was both the weirdest and the easiest. It's not easy to score a goal in the NHL. Goalies are tough, and it takes a lot to beat them. Now here was a case where I wasn't even *trying* to get a goal. My shot was nowhere near the net on purpose because I was just executing the most ordinary of tactics.

This time, none of that mattered. I scored a goal that even Gretzky, with his millions of goals, probably never scored. A wild bounce off the glass into an empty net. I raised my stick and got congratulated, but all I could think was *I sure wouldn't mind getting more of those kinds of goals.*

It didn't end there. Back then, David Letterman used to show short clips on his show that he thought were funny. A few nights later he showed that goal, and he got a good laugh out of it.

It just goes to show you can work your ass off for years, hone your skills, and play great hockey, and the thing that makes you famous is some weird bounce off a metal post. No doubt about it: hockey, and fame, can be a crazy ride.

MY BACK INJURY

In my eighth year of pro, I was playing for the Black-hawks, and we were in the playoffs against Toronto. I was in the game, and there was clear ice between me and Toronto's goal. That meant I had a chance at a breakaway, so I took off, skating hard toward the net.

One of my teammates had to pass me the puck to make the breakaway happen. He saw I was open, but he was being rushed, so the pass came to me a bit slow. I had to twist to try to catch the pass on my stick or my skate, so I was in an awkward position, not really ready to receive a pass, but I thought I could get the puck in a hurry and continue in to try for a goal.

Instead I got hit hard by a Toronto player, and I went down. I couldn't get up. Something bad had happened. I knew that right away because I couldn't feel my legs.

My teammates clustered around me, and the trainer came to take a look at me. I was scared that I couldn't feel my legs. They took me off the ice on a stretcher, and I got transported to the hospital.

Doctors there pressed on the bottoms of my feet to see if I had an appropriate neural response. I had none. Zero response.

If I was scared before, I was now completely terrified. Never mind if my hockey career was over. What if I couldn't walk anymore? By this time I was married with three kids. I couldn't afford to not be functional. I had to be healthy for them.

In the hospital, they gave me a shot of morphine and got me set up to take some x-rays. I remember I was still in my hockey uniform, pads and jersey and so on, and as usual my jersey was kind of tied up or bunched up, so they had a hard time taking it off to do the x-ray. The x-ray tech didn't want to cut the sweater.

I kind of lost it then. "There's nothing holy about it," I yelled at them. "Just get some scissors and cut the fucking sweater!"

So they did. I guess they didn't want to fight me. I don't blame them. I had the rage. Not for fighting but just out of fear.

They did the x-ray, and the upshot was that I had a broken back. They kept me in the hospital for a while. I didn't know if I was now going to have to be in a wheelchair or what. It was one of the scariest times in my life.

But as the days went by and they kept testing the bottoms of my feet, things started to improve. I could actually feel things in my legs. That was great. A few days later, I was able to gingerly stand. Not like I did before—it was awkward and painful—but I was standing. Fantastic.

After that things improved. Slowly, for sure, but they did improve. The team was out of the playoffs, so it was now the offseason. That was good news. If I was going to be recovering from a big injury, it was better to do it then than during a season. I could get the proper amount of rest for my injury to heal properly.

Things did improve, but I felt like I always had a knife blade sticking in my back. Sometimes it was tolerable, but other times it was less so. I remember I had to be careful how I moved. I could drive a car, but getting in and out was sometimes a challenge. I would park, open the door, and put one leg out, and then I'd feel an excruciating pinch in my back, the knife blade that had become my constant companion. That seized me up, and I couldn't move for something like twenty minutes. I'd be there that long, waiting for the pain to subside enough for me to get out of the car.

The summer went on like that, with me steadily improving but not really getting in playing shape. The knife in my back would come up at times I didn't expect and at times when it was very inconvenient, like when I needed to attend to my kids. They might be just a few feet away, but I couldn't get to them because of the pain. My wife and I had a three-month-old baby, a one-year-old and a three-year-old. They needed their father, but I felt like I wasn't there for them. That felt bad.

When the summer was over, I was still in no shape to play. That didn't feel good either. I wanted to contribute. I wanted to be out on the ice, but I couldn't do it, and I felt like I wasn't even part of the team anymore.

They wanted to put pins in my back and told me it was a great new surgery and I could be back playing in six months instead of nine. Years later, my daughter Ellie was injured playing rugby. I went to her neurologist with her. I asked her doctor if they still did that surgery that required putting pins in your back. He told me they didn't do that surgery anymore because it didn't work out so well.

Guess I was lucky I didn't let them do it on me back then. Eventually, I found another doctor who told me I should build up my stomach and back muscles. That would help keep the vertebrae in place, and within six to nine months, I should be much better.

Now that was something I could do. I started a regimen of sit-ups and back exercises, working to strengthen those muscles. Within three weeks, the knife was gone from my back. After a year in pain, it felt like a miracle, and maybe it was. That doctor knew what he was talking about. There was no lingering pain at all. None.

By this time it was near the end of the season. We were set to compete in the playoffs, so I thought I would see if I was in playing shape. I went out on the ice and just skated. I started out slow, but each day I ramped up the effort and skated a little bit harder, then a little bit harder after that. Eventually I was skating flat out, at my top speed, and I felt good about it.

Then one day, while I was skating up the ice, the old knife blade returned and seized me with terrible pain. I barely got off the ice and made it home. That was a lesson. I felt better, but I still had to be careful. I didn't play in that year's playoffs. I used the summer to keep up my stomach and back muscle exercises, and the knife blade stayed mostly away.

At training camp the next season, I felt I was ready to play, but I still had some doubts about the coming season. I was sure I could skate, pass, and shoot, but what about the fighting? I'd pissed off a lot of players in the league over the years. I was able to do skating and shooting drills, but that was only part of my game. Was I in shape to do the fighting game? I was pretty sure I still had the rage, but could my back stand up to the violence of getting yanked around during fights? That was a different matter.

I didn't know, but I needed to know. After we did our training one day, I asked Gary Nylund to come over. Gary was a good friend, and he was going to be my defense partner for the coming season.

"We need to wrestle on the ice," I said.

Gary looked a little puzzled.

"I need to know if my back can stand up to it," I said.

"Okay," said Gary. "I get it."

So for the next few minutes, we made like we were getting ready to fight, like when two guys grab each other's jerseys and push each other around. I let Gary toss me around like I was a ragdoll. Maybe that was a dangerous thing to do, but I had to know what I could take and what I couldn't.

I was scared my back would seize up in the middle of a fight, and I'd end up being a punching bag for the other guy. That thought terrified me because the other guy, whoever he might be, all hopped up on rage, was not going to stop fighting just because my injury asserted itself.

The good news was that even after getting pushed around by Gary, my back felt okay. I was ready to play.

That season I missed about twenty games or so. I'd be going along fine for a while, and then the knife would return. I'd be in too much pain to play, and I'd miss a few games. But each time my back got better quicker, and I returned to get ice time and contribute to the team. Even though I was terrified every minute I was out there, it felt good to be back in the game. My injury got better as the season went on. I felt like I could play a few more years. It felt good to be a hockey player again.

DEEP THOUGHTS 16

AM I IN THE HALL OF FAME OR AM I JUST FULL OF SHIT?

I HAVE KIDDED WAYNE GRETZKY IN THIS BOOK ABOUT THE MIL-lions and millions of goals he scored, but I hope it's clear that I think Wayne is every bit the great player everyone knows him as.

I began playing against Wayne in junior hockey. I remember one time when I was eighteen and he was sixteen, and shockingly, he was already a phenomenal goal scorer. We were on the ice together, and he was heading across the middle of the rink when one of his players passed him the puck.

Only this time the pass was a little behind him and a little slow, which meant he was momentarily thrown off his game, and that gave me an opportunity to hit him mid-ice. Maybe the only successful open-ice hit I ever made.

I guess I hit Wayne with his head down or in an awkward position and knocked him out cold. For my part, it was a clean hit, just a regular check for once. Nothing dirty about it, and I didn't receive a penalty. For Wayne, I'm pretty sure he never got hit like that again in his entire career. Given that, maybe I should be in the Hall of Fame for knocking out the Great One?

Another encounter with Wayne happened a few years later when we were both in the NHL. He got the puck right in front of the net at point-blank range, and it was just me between him and the goalie. He wound up for a slap shot. All I could do was stand there and try to block the shot. There was no time for anything else.

Well, Wayne must have thought point-blank range was not point blank enough because instead of taking the shot, he faked it and then pulled the puck back and began to go around me. Any other player in that situation, at such close range, would have taken the shot. I did not expect anything else.

But Wayne wasn't any other player. When he started going around me, he caught me completely flat-footed. His fake should have worked. It *would* have worked, except for one thing. I managed to feebly stick my foot out, and the puck just barely caught the toe of my skate and stopped.

Holy shit. I just deprived Wayne Gretzky of his four millionth goal. Hopefully that's not a sore spot with him to this day and he can still sleep at night. It wasn't personal, Wayne. It was just hockey.

But again, I kept one of Wayne's goals from going in. Shouldn't that put me in the Hall of Fame? Maybe. Maybe not.

Here's another Gretzky story.

I was playing for Chicago, and we were in a preseason game with Edmonton on their ice. As luck would have it, I got Wayne against the boards and hit him pretty hard, maybe a little too hard. I was actually surprised at this turn of events because Wayne was a very smart and aware player. He *always* knew where every player was, and he avoided getting hit like I'd just hit him.

Now the thing about hitting Wayne hard is that doing so will piss off his teammates, and they will come after you. Even in a preseason game, a game that meant nothing, intimidation still ruled, and I was ready for the retaliation.

Later in the game, the puck was going toward their end, and I followed it. Gretzky was behind me, too far to get at the puck, but all of a sudden, he turned on the speed and came at me fast. I could see out of the corner of my eye that his stick was high. What was he doing? Was he coming after me? Was he getting ready to hit me? That was not Wayne's style, so what was going on?

I found out soon enough. In the blink of an eye, when he was about six feet behind me, he jumped up and fell down on the ice. His stick and gloves and helmet went flying, and he laid out on the ice like he was half dead.

I never touched him. I never laid a glove or a finger on him. But it sure *looked* like I did. The guy executed a very theatrical and very convincing fake. Gotta hand it to him.

Next thing I knew, the four other Oilers on the ice were coming after me. I had seen this movie before. When four guys gang up on one guy, it can get bad very quickly. I put up my stick to cross-check them as they got closer. But two of them got my stick tangled up so I couldn't use it anymore. I yanked my hands out of my gloves, and I just started swinging. One against four.

Things got a little blurry after that. I know I connected a few times. I cut Kevin Lowe with one of my punches and he had to get stitches, but as all this was happening, I began to realize the whole thing was a put-on.

Gretzky didn't do his fake on his own. The coach and all the other players were in on it. They wanted me to draw a penalty for nothing by getting the refs to think I hit Wayne dirty when I didn't even hit him at all.

The upshot is that I did get a penalty. Wayne's trick fooled the officials. And Kevin got a bunch of stitches he did not need. All this in an exhibition game that didn't even count for anything.

So should I be in the Hall of Fame for getting penalized for a hit on Wayne Gretzky that never happened? Maybe. Maybe not.

Okay. Then listen to this next Wayne Gretzky story. I have told this story many times over the years, even when I had very little to do with hockey.

I was with the Flyers, playing in Edmonton. We were on a power play, and I was out on the ice. Wayne was penalty killing. We were losing by one goal, so we had a good chance to tie the game. Before the puck dropped, the coach yelled out, "Don't let Gretzky score!"

Did I mention this was *our* power play? Edmonton was short-handed, but the coach felt it was important for us to know we shouldn't let Gretzky score on *our* power play. Come on. Our team had already held Wayne to three goals that game. We *had* this.

You cannot make this shit up. At least I can't. Or can I?

Anyway, at the time Gretzky was on track to set one of his million records. Years before, Maurice Richard had scored fifty goals in fifty games. This was a remarkable achievement, and a lot of people in hockey figured no one was ever going to match it. They called it the unbreakable record.

Well, going into this game I'm talking about, Gretzky had forty-four goals in only thirty-nine games. He had scored three goals on us that night for a total of forty-seven goals. He was easily on track to match and surpass Richard.

With just a couple of minutes left in the game and down one goal, we pulled our goaltender to give us an extra attacker on the ice. It's a risky move that doesn't always pay off, but we had nothing to lose, so we went for it.

They dropped the puck. We pressed hard. The puck bounced around. We had it. They had it. We tried to get a shot on goal, but the puck ended up on an Oiler's stick.

Can you guess whose?

Wayne picked up the puck, took it down the ice, and scored on our empty net. I was following behind him, too far away to do anything. Too bad.

We were down two goals, and we put our goalie back in and went on with the game. Damn if we then didn't score with less than a minute to go. We were down one goal again. What did we do? What else? We pulled the goalie again.

What happened? Same thing. Wayne got the puck and scored an empty-net goal. He now had forty-nine goals.

We put our goalie back in and resumed play. I can hardly believe it as I write this down, but with thirty seconds left in the game, Wayne scored *again*. This was just a crazy game.

Half a minute left. We were down one goal. I think you know what we did. We pulled our goalie again. And I think you can probably guess what happened a *third* time. Gretzky got the puck and scored on our empty net.

I have told this story a hundred times. The guy got six goals that night, crushing Richard's record. Really, he shattered it because Wayne got his fifty goals in just thirty-nine games. Truly amazing.

Each time he scored an empty-net goal, I was behind him, chasing.

Given all that, I have to assume that there is a picture of Wayne scoring his fiftieth goal and setting a new record. And I have to figure that picture is in the Hall of Fame. And I also have to assume that I am in that picture because I was close behind him, futilely chasing him. Not close enough to stop him, but close enough to be in the picture.

I was on the ice when Gretzky got his record. Does that put me in the Hall of Fame?

I haven't been there to look, and I don't even know if that picture is there, but it should be. Which means maybe I am in the Hall of Fame. Or am I just full of shit?

I'll let you ponder the question while I tell you the rest of the story.

For years this was pretty much the only hockey story I told. The time I was on the ice with Wayne Gretzky when he achieved one of his amazing records.

As I was putting this book together, I did very little fact-checking but still found out a few things. First, before the game Wayne had forty-five goals on the season, not forty-four.

Second, he scored only two empty-net goals that night. He did not score three. We had, after all, held him to three goals prior to the empty-netters.

Third, and maybe most important, I was not even on the ice when Wayne got his record. I was on the bench. Maybe I was on the ice for his other empty-net goal and remembered it as me being on the ice for his record.

It's been forty years since that happened. I told the story wrong so many times that it became my truth. In my mind, it *was* the truth.

Stories can take over and become their own thing, bigger than the people who were in them or the ones who tell them. Like me.

It's one reason the subtitle of this book includes the words "mostly true." I have been as faithful to the truth as I can be, but I'm sure I got things wrong here and there. Memory plays crazy games with your head sometimes. What you remember is occasionally what you made up. It isn't lying. It's just the way the brain works.

It doesn't change the fact that this is still a great story. Wayne scored five goals on us. Two of them were empty net. That is a good night's work for him and kind of humiliating for us, but that's the kind of player Gretzky was.

So the answer to this deep thought is yes, I was full of shit.

BOB PROBERT: WHY DIDN'T HE KICK MY ASS?

IF YOU STAY IN THE LEAGUE LONG ENOUGH, THERE IS GOING to be some younger player coming up who will be strong and fresh, possess more rage, and be young enough to wipe you out. In my last year in the pros, just a couple of months before my final game, I figured that guy would be Bob Probert. You met him in the second paragraph of this book. Bob was a younger me.

At that time he played left wing for Detroit. Later he had several years with the Blackhawks, but that was after I left. One game against Detroit, I went after their captain, Steve Yzerman, excessively hard into the boards. As expected, Bob, who was on the ice at the time, felt he had to protect his captain, so he came after me.

By that time, Probert had already established a reputation as a tough fighter. He was one of the best fighters ever. I'd seen him on video a few times, and he had fought some of my teammates.

He squared off with Gary Nylund, who was an excellent fighter and did not give up. A brawl was going on around them during their fight, and the officials were not there to break them up. Gary kept punching Bob, and Bob held back a little. The fight went way longer than a normal hockey fight should. Gary became exhausted and kind of ran out of gas, but Bob bided his time, and when Gary started flagging, Bob amped up the hits and just started wailing on Gary.

The point is, he had the rage and the skills. He knew when to hold back and when to start hitting. He was me, back when I was younger.

Given all that, I was prepared for a scary fight, even though this was the year after my back injury and I wasn't quite back to normal. I didn't have the same strength in my body. Once you get a really serious injury, even if you come back, you're never the same. I sure didn't feel like I was back to full power. It didn't matter. I was out there, and I wasn't going to back down.

Bob and I squared off. I got my signature grip on his elbow, but damned if he didn't do the same thing on my elbow. We were practically twins as far as strategy went.

I began swinging at him but not connecting because he had a good grip on me. I tried breaking the grip by swinging my right hand forward and yanking back, but I wasn't connecting. His grip was too strong, and he didn't let go. I kept trying, though, and it was beginning to look like a repeat of his fight with Gary, where I did all the work and wore myself out and he saved his energy until I was too weak to put up any kind of effective defense.

This went on for a while. I summoned the rage for one last swing and tried to hit him, but his grip caused my punch to fall short. He did not hit back. So I did it again. I amped up the rage and took another last swing, which didn't connect. I think during our standoff, I connected with maybe half a punch out of a dozen or so swings.

As this was going on, I thought, *What am I thinking? Why am I out here trying to fight this guy?*

After all, I didn't have to hit Yzerman into the boards. I didn't have to try to throw punches at Bob Probert. I didn't have to do any of that. I could have left Yzerman alone. When Bob came after me, I could have just held onto his sweater, like he was holding onto mine, and we could have wrestled on the ice for a few seconds, let the officials pull us apart, and gone on our ways. That would have been the smart thing.

But I was a fighter. It was what I was primed to do, so I tried to do it.

To this day, I don't know why Bob Probert did not throw a punch at me or why he didn't even try to throw a punch. He was a fighter who chose not to fight on that occasion. How was he avenging my hit on Yzerman by not swinging? I can speculate forever about the reason. But that's all it would be: speculation.

FACE SHIELDS AND THE BULLSHIT OF UNWRITTEN RULES

WITH ABOUT TWO MONTHS TO GO BEFORE I RETIRED, I GOT CUT around my eyes three different times, each occasion needing stitches.

On one of those times, the guy was trying to skate around me, and I hooked him, a basic play completely expected and allowed in that situation. The guy exaggerated my hook, made it look worse than it was, and spun around with his stick high and tried to make it look accidental, but it was intentional. His stick connected with my face right near my eye.

By that time I had survived a lot of shit. Concussions, cuts, a broken back, and more. I did not want to end my career blind, and with all this damage near my eye sockets, it seemed almost inevitable that I was going to suffer something major around my eye.

I told our trainer I wanted to start wearing a face shield and asked if he would get one for me. These were clear panes of plastic that attached to the front edge of the helmet and came about halfway down the face. They protected the eyes and the nose. They are very common today, but not so common when I was playing.

Back then, the unwritten rule was that goal scorers could wear face shields, and some of them did. But fighters? That was a different story. Tough guys did not wear face shields.

I have to say, though, that my eyeballs were just as soft and vulnerable as anyone else's, including superstars and goal scorers. We were all created equal in that regard.

It didn't matter to management. I got my face shield and started wearing it at practice. Within seconds the coach got steaming mad.

"You wearing that only in practice?" he asked.

"No," I said.

"You're going to wear it during *games*?"

"Yes, I am."

More steam came shooting out of his ears, like I had ignited a fire in his head. I guess he thought if I wore a shield, I was not going to get into fights. That was the basic reason fighters were not supposed to wear shields, I think.

Hell, if a fight erupted I could fight with a shield, no problem. But I guess he didn't see it that way. He thought I was not going to be as tough as I would be without the shield. But maybe even more important than all that, I was breaking the unwritten rule that fighters did not wear shields.

I didn't care. I wore the shield. I expected pushback, but surprisingly, they didn't fight me on it too much. They didn't like it, but I wore my shield, and I loved it. There's a reason players nowadays use those shields. They do a good job protecting their faces.

I don't know if wearing mine saved my eyes or not, but I was glad to have it as extra protection. That was the best unwritten rule I could have broken.

DEEP THOUGHTS 17

SCOUTING REPORTS: OUR SECRET WEAPON

UP UNTIL MY LATER YEARS IN THE PROS, WE DIDN'T HAVE scouting reports. As players, we all knew other players, and we had a very good idea of how they all played, their strengths, and their weaknesses. We knew the good passers, the good shooters, the speedsters, the tough guys, and so on.

If a player came up from the minors for an opposing team and you didn't know anything about him, all you had to do was ask around, and there would inevitably be someone who played him in junior or the minors, and you could get intel from them.

Nothing wrong with that system. It worked.

But to gain competitive advantages, we needed advanced intel. Management started sending scouts out to games that featured teams we were to play in the next few days or so.

I remember one of the first such scouting reports I saw. It went like this: "Their goaltender is hot. Make sure you get in front of him and get a lot of shots on goal."

Fair enough. Made sense.

This is the next scouting report I saw, for a different team: "Their goaltender is not hot. Make sure you get in front of him and get a lot of shots on goal."

What can I say? Genius. Pure genius.

It didn't end with goaltenders. Here's another report: "Their star defenseman is playing really well. You gotta make sure to hit him and put a lot of pressure on him." Another report a week later: "Their defensemen are not playing well. You gotta make sure to hit them and put a lot of pressure on them."

I really don't know what else they could have said. Hockey prowess comes from the imagination of skilled players. It's hard to put that into a scouting report. Better players played better. There. That's a good report. You can take that to the bank.

These reports were not exactly useful to us as far as helping us figure out strategy during a game, but they did provide us all with some entertainment. After games we went over them to each other over a few beers and laughed our asses off.

I remember one report we read said one forward didn't like getting hit. I made like I was talking to the coach. "Hey, coach," I said, "can we have a list of guys who *like* getting hit?"

Laughter ensued. Hysterics went on and on as we read these truly useless scouting reports to each other. I guess, looking back, maybe the point was to give us some entertainment and a few laughs.

GLORY BE: WE FINALLY HAVE A RATING SYSTEM

IN MY TENTH YEAR AS A PRO, PLAYING FOR THE BLACKHAWKS, our coach decided we needed a rating system. He was going to rate each of us on a scale of one to five—one being the best and five being the worst—for every game. What motivated this, I have no idea. It seemed like a remarkably useless thing to do.

That's because *everyone* knew who the best players in any game were. And everyone knew how well they were playing. They were the ones who scored goals or got assists, killed penalties, manufactured scoring chances by giving good passes, intimidated the opposing team with hard hits, and so on. I am pretty sure we didn't need a rating system to know that.

I always got rated a three or a four. Every single game for the entire season. This was ludicrous in itself. Not because I thought I was necessarily the superior player on the team, but if I was always below average, why was I always out there on the ice against the other team's premier line? Why was I carrying a lot of playing minutes? No explanation for that.

But I guess I was just a hockey player and did not understand the intricacies of management and coaching. I chalked the whole idea up to some sort of double reverse demotivating confidence destroyer. Like maybe if I kept getting a low rating, I would up my game.

As though I wasn't already doing the drills every practice, working on keeping in shape, going out on the ice full bore every time, checking and hustling, breaking up the other team's plays, and going into corners to mix it up with their guys. I was doing all that and more. All of us were. There were no slackers on our team, so what was up with my low scores? Other players received good scores all the time. What was going on? Beats me.

I remember one time Glen Cochrane was out on the ice and got into a fight with Bob Probert, who I already talked about as a fierce fighter. Glen squaring off with him was a big deal. Glen did his best, but Probert was exceptionally tough, and from my perspective, Probert got the better of Glen in that fight.

Glen played one shift that game, the shift in which he fought Probert. The coach gave him a rating of one for the game. I agreed with that rating for Glen in that game. Anyone who challenged Probert to a fight deserved the highest rating, so no argument from me.

Sometime later, I got into a fight with Probert. I threw about twenty hard punches and unfortunately hit him with about a half a punch, and he threw none at me. It would be hard to argue that I did not at least draw that fight. In addition, I played the whole game. I got lots of ice time and worked hard every shift. After the game, I got my report card from the coach and saw I was rated a four. Only one rating point above the worst possible rating.

All I can say is holy fucking shit.

Normally I would have just noted this BS and moved on. After all, there wasn't much I could do about it. The team owned me, and they had their ways. They weren't going to listen to me.

But at that time I had only a couple of months till the end of my NHL career. I didn't want to let this go. And worse, I could afford to not let this go. The truth is, I could have coasted those last few games. I didn't have to fight Probert. But I didn't coast. I kept playing my absolute best for my own personal pride and for my teammates. To get such a low rating for a pretty good game was wrong, and for once I wasn't going to let it go.

By that time I was pretty fed up with the culture of coaching. From the time I was seven years old when a coach yelled at me and threatened to cut me to all the times coaches told me I was wrong to go left and wrong to go right, not to mention all the times they didn't play me for some petty reasons I wasn't privy to, all of it just kind of welled up in me, and I figured it was about time I tried to understand this reverse demotivating confidence destroyer psychology.

Better late than never, I guess.

So the next day, instead of going directly to practice and doing the drills, I first went to Bob Pulford's office. Who better to explain the psychology of demotivating players than the general manager?

"Dr. Bob," I said, "I got a four for last night's game where I fought Bob Probert." I showed him my report card.

"Okay," said Bob.

"A while ago, Glen got into a fight with Probert and lost. And that was the only shift he had all game. And he got a one rating."

Bob didn't say anything. He was in a spot. I was telling him the rating system was unfair, and he had to agree just based on what I just told him. On the other hand, he had to defend his coach. That was part of his job.

I had never been in this position before. I had never challenged a general manager or a coach before that day.

"What would it have taken for me to get a three in that game?" I asked him.

Bob was stymied. As I've said before, I had a lot of respect for Bob. I thought he was a great general manager and a standup guy, but he had no answers for me that day.

"Or did I get a one for fighting that game and a seven (below the rating chart) for the rest of the game, so the coach averaged it out and I got a four? Is that how it works?"

I went on like that for a while, coming up with wild scenarios about how the rating system actually worked. I was having fun with

Bob. I am pretty sure he didn't see it that way, but crossing the line and confronting management was exhilarating. It felt great to be an asshole for the day.

I couldn't have done this earlier. Previously, they owned me and my future. One word from them, and I could have lost my career. But not anymore. It's funny what getting near the end of a career can do for your courage. Take this job and—well, you know.

The best part of all this was when we went on the road a few days later. After one of the games, the players were sharing a few beers, and I told them about my meeting with Dr. Bob. They just about died laughing when I told them what I said. First because the whole rating system was stupid and deserved a stupid confrontation like I had with Bob.

And second because no one, I mean *no one* ever dared to talk to management like I did. I don't think I ever had a better time telling a story.

SMOKING IS FUN!

THE RATING SYSTEM WAS NOT THE ONLY INSTANCE WHERE I felt like I could defy management in those last couple of months. Not that I was starting a revolution or anything. It was just that I was tired of all the nonsense they kept throwing at us, and I was willing to give some back for once.

To set the scene, whenever the coach wanted to talk to us on the ice, we were to get down on one knee and look up at him. A lot of guys had bad knees. A lot of guys wore knee braces. Getting down on one knee was painful for a lot of the team, me included. We didn't need that, but that was what our coach wanted, so we did it. I hated it.

So one day we were all down on one knee, and the coach said he had an important announcement.

"We've got three guys who've made the commitment to making our team a better team."

I didn't know what he was getting at. Everyone was always working to make the team better, but I kept my mouth shut and remained on my sore knee and listened.

The coach continued. "Denis Savard, Steve Larmer, and Rick Vaive have all agreed to stop smoking."

I sure had nothing against people stopping smoking. The dressing room was often filled with smoke as players puffed away between periods or before games. I sometimes had a hard time getting good air in the dressing room, especially with my allergies. Smoking is mostly frowned upon today, but back then it was a different culture, and smoking was allowed in many places you would never see it today.

I don't know how the team talked these three players into stopping smoking. Did they get together and present their quitting smoking plan to the players? No idea. I just know we were all supposed to clap and congratulate these three guys for quitting smoking.

But I wasn't in the mood. By that time I was beginning to feel the strain of playing hockey, and things were different in my life. I had three kids. I was away from home at least three days a week, on the road playing games, and I was missing my family. I wanted to be a great father, but when I came home, my kids were talking or taking their first steps, or having some other milestone, and I had no idea what was going on with them because I was gone so much of the time. My wife was alone in a city where she had no family, looking after three little kids twenty-four hours a day.

My playing life was great. I loved all the guys on my team, and I still loved playing hockey. But my personal life, with my family commitments, was changing. It was all just starting to feel wrong.

Anyway, all of that was on my head as pain shot up my knee and my coach was feeding us some dumb story about quitting smoking. And I got to thinking. These three guys were literally our three top scorers. And they smoked. So I opened my big mouth.

"Maybe the better plan," I said, "is for the rest of us to *start* smoking. Then we could be top scorers like them."

The whole team laughed. They loved my comment. I had this grin on my face, and the coach glared at me. I had just undermined everything he'd said, but, come on. The general manager was a smoker, and he was okay with smoking in the dressing room, so what was all this malarkey about improving the team by guys quitting smoking?

It almost made leaning on my sore knee worth it. Almost.

The coach always gave me a poor rating, so he didn't think much of me, but at that moment I was pretty sure he hated me. That was okay. What was I afraid of? A five rating? Ouch!

I knew I couldn't be saying these things without hurting my career, but I was retiring soon, and it was fun. For me at least.

MY SHOUT-OUTS TO MARIO LEMIEUX AND WAYNE GRETZKY

I'VE BEEN OUT OF THE GAME FOR A LONG TIME, OBVIOUSLY. SO I am not familiar with today's players. I can only comment on players of my era. I've talked about some of them in these pages, and I hope I've done well by them and showed you exactly how and why I thought they were great.

But I saved the best for last.

In my opinion, Mario Lemieux and Wayne Gretzky were so far above everyone else in the league it was like they were playing something other than hockey. I never figured out what that game was.

The scouting reports on both of these guys were that we were supposed to make sure they didn't get any breakaways. For both of them, breakaways were not some kind of fluke. They got breakaways again and again and again, as though it was perfectly natural.

They had bucketloads of anticipation. They always knew where players were and where they were going. They always knew where the puck was and where *it* was going. And then they would be there, ready to take it in for a shot on goal. There was little you could do to stop these guys, and I never figured out their game. Neither did most of the rest of the league, which is why they racked up such impressive career numbers for goals and assists.

To top it all off, and this is the worst part of all, both Wayne and Mario are just about the nicest guys you would ever want to meet.

In my considered opinion, they should have literally been in a league of their own. The Lemieux-Gretzky league where they were the only two players. They were not playing the same game the rest of us were playing. At the very least, they should have been *penalized* for not playing what the rest of us were playing.

PART 5

FINALLY SAYING NO

A TOUGH DECISION

MOST GUYS RETIRED WHEN THEY DIDN'T GET ANOTHER CONtract. Their team didn't want them anymore and no other team wanted them either, so no contract equaled end of career.

There could be any number of reasons for this. If you got an injury that adversely affected your play, no contract. If your goal scoring was way down from what it had been, no contract. Basically, if management thought you couldn't contribute to the success of the team, then you didn't get a contract renewal, and you were out of the game or traded to another team if another team wanted you. Which was certainly not guaranteed.

Playing pro sports takes stamina, strength, drive, and ability. Those things don't always last. The average length of a career in all professional sports, not just hockey, is less than four years.

This means every player knows their time is coming.

In my case, after my tenth year in the NHL and my fifth year with Chicago, they *did* offer to renew my contract. They wanted me. That was very tempting.

But.

I had exhausting allergies that made me tired every game. I had a back injury that was still giving me problems. And I had hip pain that was always there.

On the other hand, my back injury was getting better. And I had played my whole career with the allergies and the hip pain. I could deal with those. I knew if I stayed in shape, I could probably go on for another five years and maybe even longer than that.

As I've said many times in this book, you never say you can't play. It was drilled into my head and into my very being that I was *always* ready to play. I would *always* say yes to a practice, a shift, a fight, a game, and a season. Always.

Everything I had been taught about how to play the game and how to be in the game and how to contribute told me I should keep playing. I should say yes to this offer.

But.

Things were different from when I started. I had a family. I was married with three daughters. My oldest was about to start kindergarten. I wanted stability for my family, and if I played another year for Chicago, there was no guarantee that I was not going to be traded in the middle of the season and have to leave that day, and we would all be uprooted and have to move to an unfamiliar city. Not to mention all the logistics of the move would fall on my wife's shoulders. That was not something I wanted to do to my wife and kids.

I wanted to be a great dad and a great husband. I couldn't do that when I was on the road half the year with my team. I couldn't do that when I came home with a scarred and stitched-up face that scared my little girls.

Don't get me wrong. I absolutely *loved* playing hockey. It was the major part of my life up until then. I loved the competition. I loved being on a team with such a great bunch of guys. I took a lot of pride in being a good defenseman and working with my defense partner to protect our goalie and our team. I could have done all that for the rest of my life.

I knew how hockey worked. I knew where I was in the hierarchy. I knew the rules of both games, and I played them both well.

At the same time, there were things I did not care for. I hated getting yelled at by coaches. The constant travelling got old. I hated being hurt. I even hated playing hurt and then getting yelled at for not playing well. All of that took away from the joy of the game.

When I weighed all that against the well-being of my family, there was no question what I should do. I turned down the contract and left hockey.

I said no to the next season and every season after that. I finally said no to every practice, shift, and game.

I have no doubt I made the right decision, although at the time it was scary. The Blackhawks were offering me good money to play another few seasons with them. It didn't matter. I had built some business skills and made lots of business connections on all those offseasons over the years, and I thought I had a chance to be a good businessman and entrepreneur, someone who could provide for my family. It wasn't guaranteed by any means, but I was ready to enter the abyss, which was what I felt opened up under me when I made my decision to say no.

It took some mental adjustment. Actually, a lot of mental adjustment. What was my life without hockey in it? At first it was tough. I remember as the summer after my last season started winding down to Labor Day, it felt weird not to be getting into playing shape. It felt weird that I was not going to be practicing with my teammates. After all, many, many of my friends were in hockey.

When the season got going, my old teammates sometimes invited me to hang out with them after a game, but that didn't happen till late at night, eleven o'clock or even later. That didn't fit with my non-playing life, so I turned down those chances, and after a while I didn't get asked anymore.

I followed my old team's games on television sometimes, and when I did I was *in* the game. I rooted for my guys, worried about them getting hit, and was right there with the defensemen cutting down the angles and setting up to block shots. My heart was in the game even though I was nowhere near the game.

That soon tapered off as my daughters were not interested in watching hockey with me. Then, as the years went by and the players were no longer familiar, I sometimes watched games, but I wasn't in them anymore. Eventually I became a spectator, and hockey was something in my past, a different life. The game moved on with new players, new teams, and a new culture.

I moved on too. I started and sold dozens of businesses. I got my pilot's license and have flown all over the world in my plane.

But most of all, after hockey, I spent as much time as I could with my kids. I coached their sports teams and was as involved in their lives as possible. I may not have achieved my ambition of being a *great* dad, but I do know I tried my very hardest, and I left nothing on the table in terms of effort. I guess you'd have to ask them about that if you wanted to know the unvarnished truth.

I still have all my memories of playing hockey. I've told some of those stories here. I have a lot more that I didn't tell, but a book has only so many pages.

I do remember my last game.

We were in the first round of playoffs against St. Louis. We were losing badly. I had already decided this was my last season, even though I had not told anyone yet. I wanted to play out the season without that thought in their heads.

I could have coasted. I could have refused to go into the corners, maybe held back a little on my hits. I could even have said my laces were broken and I had to go into the dressing room for twenty minutes to replace them. I could have done all that. Nothing would have happened. Nothing would have changed. We were still going to lose the game and the series.

But I couldn't do any of that. I was out there to play, and I played just as hard as I did in any game I ever played, which is to say I gave it my all, skated as hard and as fast as I could, blocked shot after shot, and just had the time of my life playing the game I loved.

After we lost the game and we were all in the dressing room, a sad feeling around us because our season was over, I sat, trying to accept that it was all really over. It didn't seem right, in a way. I was still strong, still capable. I could have kept playing.

The next day, all the guys got together, and we had a few beers, talked about the season, and had some laughs. I told some of my closest teammates that I was done. This was my last season. That was a sad moment. It was my goodbye to hockey and to some of my best friends.

Later, after most of the guys had left, Keith Brown and Curt Fraser stayed behind with me.

"What are you going to do now?" they asked.

The whole thing was weird because it was my decision. Most guys leave when someone else decides. The team owner, the coach, or the general manager. Or all three. In a lot of ways, it would have been easier to have been traded or cut.

I didn't have an answer for them then. I didn't know.

But things worked out just fine. I loved hockey, but I loved my family more. Life after hockey has been good for us. I never regretted leaving, but I do remember some of the good times and bad times I had playing a game that is close to the hearts of so many people.

It was a grand time, and I wouldn't have missed any of it.

ACKNOWLEDGMENTS

AS I LOOK BACK, THERE ARE SO MANY PEOPLE WHO HAVE INFLU-enced me, some in small ways, some in large ways, but all very important and special to me. I wish there was room to name them all. I was fortunate enough to call many of my heroes my friends. I am blessed.

Thanks to my wife, Rita, who has been eternally supportive, my voice of reason, who makes me a better person. And who is kind enough to remind me to put the trash out every Monday and Thursday.

Thanks to my daughter Ellie Neiberger for insight and perspective. You got me going on this memoir with Mad Writing. I wouldn't have gotten started without you.

Thanks to my daughter Kristie Dudley. With a relentlessly positive attitude, you pushed me to do one interview, my first in almost forty years, that inspired this book.

Thanks to my daughter Victoria Wilson, for rewriting a chapter of my book and showing me that the book could be fun and enjoyable.

Thanks to Mario Milosevic for making me seem smarter than I am and for keeping my story coherent.

Thanks to Ellie Cole for keeping stuff positive and moving me ahead in this book-writing process, even when I seemed determined to fight hard to remain stuck in a rabbit hole.

Thanks to Lance for inspiring me to be completely candid with my story.

Thanks to Natasha. I am eternally grateful to you for advising me to not listen to Lance.

9 781544 551258